Going Solo
Creating your freelance editorial business
Second edition

Sue Littleford

First published in the UK in 2021 by
Studio 206, Milton Keynes Business Centre
Foxhunter Drive
Linford Wood
Milton Keynes
MK14 6GD

ciep.uk

Copyright © 2023 Chartered Institute of Editing and Proofreading

ISBN 978 1 838358 20 4 (print)
ISBN 978 1 838358 21 1 (PDF ebook)
ISBN 978 1 838358 29 7 (ePub)

Second edition 2021; minor revisions 2023

Revised first edition 2020: ISBN 978 1 916437 40 1 (print),
ISBN 978 1 916437 41 8 (PDF ebook)

First edition 2016: ISBN 978 0 993129 31 5; minor revisions 2018

All rights reserved. No part of this publication may be reproduced or used in any manner without written permission from the publisher, except for quoting brief passages in a review. The moral rights of the author have been asserted.

The information in this work is accurate and current at the time of publication to the best of the author's and publisher's knowledge, but it has been written as a short summary or introduction only. Readers are advised to take further steps to ensure the correctness, sufficiency or completeness of this information for their own purposes.

Typeset in-house. Original design by Ave Design (avedesign.studio)
Image credits: Unsplash: p1 Stephan Henning; p8 Slidebean; p15 Mikey Harris; p23 dole777; p27 Amy Hirschi; p33 Russ Ward; p43 Markus Winkler; p61 Samule Sun; p62 Elena Moshvilo. Shutterstock: p5 Brian A Jackson; p53 sophiecat; p66 New Africa; p72 i_photos.

Contents

1	Introduction	1
2	Basics	3
	Business planning	3
	Marketing handouts	11
	What do you need?	12
3	Knowledge	17
	Training	17
	Mastering your tools	19
	Reference books	20
	Style guides	21
	Social media and online communities	22
	Continuing professional development	24
4	Clients	25
	Finding work	25
	Working for students	28
	Marketing and advertising	29
	Working with your clients	34
5	Records	43
	Statutory records	43
	Other essential records	45
	Desirable records	47
6	Money	48
	The importance of keeping track	48
	Income tax, National Insurance and VAT	49

Business expenses	53
Trading allowance	55
Deciding on your accounting year	55
Invoicing and chasing late payment	57
Should you be a company?	58
Do you need an accountant?	59
Bank accounts	59

7 | You 60

Taking care of yourself	60
The basic set-up	60
Time management	62
Support from others	64
Dealing with criticism and imposter syndrome	66
IT security	67
Business resilience	68
Upgrading CIEP membership and other goals	71

8 | Resources 73

References 83

1 | Introduction

This guide focuses on setting up and running your business. It assumes that you have already trained in the core editorial skills, or that you are taking care of obtaining the training you need. It is strongly recommended that you do train, although this guide can't, for reasons of space, go into detail on what to train in and where to source it. Check the CIEP website if you're looking for direction on training.

As everyone will have reached this point in their career in their own way, guidance can only be general. You may need to take formal advice on money matters, for example, tailored to your current circumstances. Tax is dictated not just by your new freelance business, but by *all* your sources of income and your personal situation.

This second edition of *Going Solo* is written as the world struggles to come to terms with the Covid-19 pandemic, and the UK enters recession. Much is expected to change, and quickly, as the UK government tries to steer the country to recovery, to negotiate the end of the Brexit transition phase and to refill its coffers. Rather than scatter caveats throughout about 'different arrangements under pandemic conditions' for events that would usually take place face to face in happier times, it is hoped that this guide will outlast the pandemic and it is phrased accordingly.

At the time of writing, the UK is also facing changes to employment status under IR35, due in April 2021; more frequent, and online, tax record-keeping and returns under Making Tax Digital (MTD), due in April 2023 for income tax (and April 2022 for *all* businesses registered for VAT); and the impact of the end of the Brexit transition is still to be revealed (from 1 January 2021).

The guide is necessarily heavily oriented towards the situation in the UK – the CIEP is based in the UK, although with an international reach and outlook; readers in other countries will need to find out the appropriate business, legal and tax arrangements required for their own location, but there should be enough pointers here towards the things you'll need to investigate in your own countries.

New for this edition, supplementary information, such as current tax rates and worked examples, is now available to CIEP members on the **CIEP website**, where content can be updated far more easily for fast-moving changes.

Even so, this edition is quite a bit longer than the previous incarnation, so if you're thinking about going solo with your own editorial business, or have recently got going, it will still help guide you through the things you'll need to consider as you set up your enterprise. As space is limited, there are lots of references to websites and other resources for you to gain fuller information. Here, I can only point you in the direction of the things you need to know about, to try to help you avoid the 'unknown unknowns'.

2| Basics

Business planning

Being a freelance editor or proofreader isn't all about sitting quietly reading brand new books before publication and being Oscar Wilde, taking all morning to remove a comma and spending all afternoon putting it back. It *is*, however, about running a business, so your business skills will be as important to your success as your editorial skills – perhaps even more so.

Everyone going into business needs a business plan.[1] Setting up your own editorial business means that you have to think through a whole bunch of questions – and a business plan is how you can record your lists of questions, your musings and your decisions, tightening it as you obtain answers and choose your direction. The document needn't be formal – you're unlikely to be applying for large business loans for plant and machinery, after all – but it does need to focus your thoughts. Thinking things through, testing out ideas while they are still ideas, trying out different approaches – all these will save you time and money when you do start to take practical steps to launch your business. Time spent thinking, and investigating, and planning, is never wasted.

I'm going to assume that you have, or are in the process of acquiring, strong editorial skills. So – what services will you offer? And to whom? The great thing about being freelance is that *you* choose. If you have a publishing background, you'll be able to use your contacts to find work, and will have a track record in a particular publishing niche that you can point to in your CV and marketing. If you're new to the publishing world – for example if this is a second career, or you have just left university – you may have skills from your old job or your course that you can reapply in your own business (and can point to in your CV and marketing, too).

> **Think like a business. Act like a business. Be a business. Right from day one; in fact, from the day you decide to get into editing/proofreading. Have a business plan, and a marketing plan, no matter how basic.**
>
> Janet MacMillan

Make no mistake, you're a business owner with obligations that HM Revenue and Customs (HMRC) will expect you to understand. So, in developing your plan, you will work out who your clients are, where you'll find them, what you want to do for them, how you're going to abide by the law, how you're going to establish yourself in your new career, how you're going to continue to nurture your skills and expertise and how you're going to look after your own wellbeing while doing so.

So – dive in.

Ask yourself:

1. What services will I offer?

Are you a copyeditor? A proofreader? A developmental editor? Two of these? All three? Have you been a project manager? Do you also index? Do you already have a publishing niche? Do you have any prior expertise? Were you in medicine or in law, or were you a teacher or an academic? Do you want to continue to use that expertise, or are you looking for a complete break? Received wisdom says that people with a distinct area of expertise will find work more readily in that field and may well find it pays better.

2. Am I a specialist or a generalist?

Is your specialism by subject matter or by skill? What kind of demand is there for your specialism? What kind of competition is there from people offering similar skills and knowledge? Do you get bored working in one area all the time? Would you enjoy chopping and changing between varied subject matter and exercising different skills? Some people specialise – others deliberately don't. It will help you to plan if you think about how you would like to work. You get to design the business you actually want to work in, but do be realistic about how you're going to get there. You may have to take some intermediate steps to get to where you want to be – whether you still need to build up skills or you just need to be earning something, anything, in the shorter term – but you'll only get there if you know what you're aiming for.

3. Can I apply previous experience?

You have experience already that you can apply to your new business. You may be new as a business owner, but you may have a background in customer service, time management, negotiating or estimating, or you may have IT or subject-matter expertise. You may have a hobby that gives you an 'in' with a niche publisher. You may, indeed, have a publishing background! Draw on your past to inform how you run your business and to identify editorial niches that you would like to occupy, where you may have an edge over other editors and therefore capture the work. Before you say that you have no transferable skills, take a look at a blog post I wrote in 2015.[2]

4. Who is my client?

Once you know what services you will offer in your new business, you can begin to work out who your clients are. There are three broad areas:

- **Businesses and organisations:** If your background is in business, marketing, finance or administration, you may want to work with businesses and charities on annual reports, marketing materials, financial analyses and so on, or with the many quasi-governmental and supranational organisations that publish reports frequently.
- **Traditional publishers and packagers:** Work with publishers is getting harder to find, with takeovers, downsizing, outsourcing and the current move to oblige authors to arrange their own editing,

but it's still available, if not directly with the publisher, then with the prepress companies (packagers) that take the raw manuscript from the publisher and hand back files ready to go to the printer.
- **Authors and academics:** Many editorial professionals choose to work directly with authors, where there is demand, but perhaps less understanding of what editorial help is available and how to choose it wisely.

5. Where is my client?

Where do your clients hang out? Where do they find their editors and proofreaders? How are they going to hear about you and decide to hire you? How will you find out the answers to these questions?

The internet is awash with advice that authors don't need editing, or that their friends will do it free of charge. However, with the likes of Amazon taking an increasingly firm line on the technical quality of self-published works on their platform, there may be some rebound yet to come in favour of professional editing, even for indie authors.

Think all this through, dispassionately. Your answers to the five questions above will dictate how you market yourself and where you will search for clients.

Branding

You've decided what services you're going to offer, and to whom. So how are you going to convey that in your branding – the way you present your business to the world at large and potential clients in particular? Decisions include choosing a name for your business, a strapline, a logo and your colour scheme.

The name you trade under should be simple to remember, distinctive and, ideally, not used by anyone else. It could also indicate the services you offer (or at least not make them a surprise). It should certainly not riff on the name of a major company – some of their legal teams have no sense of humour and will try to force you to change your name, should they ever find out about you. Check your shortlist of potential names on the internet, to see if you're sufficiently distinctive not to lose business to an established enterprise in the same field. Also check with a domain name registrar to see if you're likely to be able to register a domain name that makes sense with your trading name. Even if you think you won't need a website, or at least not yet, do register the domain you'd want if you were going to have one, so someone else doesn't snap it up instead of you, leaving you unable to match your trading name and your domain name. Consider whether you want to register your trading name as a trademark.³

Some people support using your own name in your business name, whereas others prefer to go for something more catchy and corporate-sounding. If you know your name is one that people struggle to spell correctly, something shorter and/or simpler may be the way to go.

You'll want a logo to use on your website, your invoices and so on. You may be able to design something yourself, for example using Canva,[4] or you may prefer to hire someone who can show you a range of designs and then provide files in the formats you'll need for different uses. If you choose to hire someone, do think first about the image you want to project, the message you want to get across and the kind of colours you want to use. A designer will thank you for giving them a brief to follow – they shouldn't be expected to guess what you might want! While you're thinking about your logo, give some thought, too, to the typeface you intend to use in your communications – it's all part of your branding, and the two should work in harmony. Read up on **branding** in the Resources section.

Advertising and marketing

Now it's time to think about how you will get your name out there, in front of your preferred type of client for your preferred type of work.

I've often been told that advertising doesn't work for editorial professionals. I think that really depends on where you advertise, though. I picked up a major, long-term client when he was browsing the *Yellow Pages* (OK, it was a while ago!) looking for a local copyeditor. But you must be aware of your costs and the value for money your advertising budget is giving you. Read more on **advertising** in chapter 3.

Take a look at marketers' websites for hints and tips.[5]

Increasingly popular is content marketing, where you write helpful material – blog posts, downloads, ebooks – and post them on your website and on social media. Position yourself as a person who is there to solve a client's problems and *who is knowledgeable about how to do it*. Having great content on your website will encourage potential clients to engage with you, continues working for you long after you wrote it, and is helpful with search engine optimisation (SEO) and findability on the internet. Content marketing is more of a slow burn, but it will eventually pay off.

Budgeting and monitoring

Even if you're not yet operational, you will need to get a grasp of the money side of things. For some reason, a lot of freelancers are shy about the money. Don't be. This isn't a hobby, it's your business – the way you're going to put a roof over your head and food on the table. Be cool, calm and businesslike from the outset.

You'll start incurring expenses before you land your first client, which HMRC refers to as 'pre-trading expenses'. You'll need to record what you spend, when and on what (read more on keeping **records** in chapter 4) even though you're not yet open for business. Do exercise caution and buy only what you really need. Don't let your enthusiasm for your new enterprise see you buying every book on grammar and editing that you can find!

Starting a business from scratch is usually a long, slow haul. Some freelancers will be established sooner than others; even established freelancers experience gaps in their workflow, and therefore their cash flow. Think through *now* how you will fund yourself if you struggle to find work.

> *How you cut over to being a freelancer will dictate your budget, but as a rule of thumb, have at least half a year's salary in the bank before you go solo if you are to support yourself.*

Lack of cash flow has brought down many more businesses than lack of profits, so do take a reasonably pessimistic view as you do your sums – round up what you need to earn to make a viable living as an editor or proofreader, and to be able to weather financial storms, and round down your likely income in the first few years. The pandemic has exposed the lack of resilience of many businesses.

Many people find it beneficial, if they're currently in paid employment, to start building their business at weekends and in the evenings – very hard work, but it does mean that you're fed and housed while you discover whether you can find clients, and whether you actually enjoy the work in real life. As more freelance work comes in, it may be possible to go part-time and only become a full-time freelancer when you're confident that you have the client base to support you.

Marketing handouts

It's often useful to have something you can hand to a prospective client that tells them what you can do for them. Depending on your target market, this could be a leaflet or a CV. A leaflet allows you to say what you will do, and a CV what you have done. Both of these documents can also be placed on your website as PDF downloadables, to give your marketing materials greater reach – but do keep your personal security in mind, so don't include your full postal address, for example.

Marketing leaflets should address the problems you can solve for your client. If you're trying to acquire a client who has perhaps never thought to buy in editorial services before, helping them understand why they need you (rather than why you need them) can convince the client to at least give it a go.

Keep CVs short and up to date. Write a core CV that you can amend to suit the potential client that you're sending it to. You don't need to include your age, or anything that gives it away, such as the year you took your A levels. Don't clutter it up with personal information (marital status, number of children or hobbies, for example) *unless* it's directly relevant to the client's needs in an editorial freelancer.

Give the information in descending chronological order – have the most current, relevant information at the top, with your education at the end, if at all. The longer ago your education was, the less detail you should include. Membership of school societies 30 years ago takes up space that should be given to content that will work harder for you, as well as suggesting to the reader that you're not sure what's relevant to them.

Email your marketing materials as PDFs rather than Word documents, so you have control over how they look if they are printed out – use your branding, and make sure the documents are inviting and easy to read in terms of appearance and layout.

Keep your CV under review frequently for the first two or three years – the whole thing – as you learn what works and what doesn't. Put notes in your diary to remind you to do this review. Each time you revise it, do check it carefully (and have someone else read it closely). In this business, typos in your CV won't win you any clients. See also '**Adapting your CV**' in chapter 3.

In a marketing leaflet, you have more room to pitch your skills to your target audience and explain what you can do for them. Perhaps they are businesses that may not have considered buying in editorial expertise before, or you want to reach students and academics. Before going to the expense of having the leaflet printed, do consider how you are going to get your leaflet into the hands of the people you're targeting. By mail? Putting them through local businesses' letterboxes? Leaving them in libraries and common rooms? This will also guide you on how many copies to have printed.

What do you need?

Computer, printer and broadband

You will, of course, need a computer. Microsoft Word is the dominant program for editing. Proofreaders will need a PDF reader program. Start off with the free versions; you can upgrade to the paid ones, which are more feature-rich, if you find you need more functions to meet your clients' requirements. Copyeditors may well be expected to mark up artwork on PDFs, so they, too, should have a PDF program. CIEP members tend to use Adobe Acrobat (paid-for), Adobe Acrobat Reader (free) or PDF-XChange Editor (free).

In other chapters there are mentions of additional software. Explore these during this business planning phase so you have a shopping list for those you think you'll get good use from but have to pay for.

There is no clear winner between PCs and Macs for editorial work. Choose whichever you find most comfortable and instinctive to work on. If you have a Mac and need to run a PC-only program, then you can, by using a virtual Windows program such as Parallels.

If you've had an IT department at work to rely on, it may come as a shock to realise you're now solely responsible for IT security, backing up data and having a practical disaster recovery plan so that if your computer dies, your client's deadline doesn't. One of the greatest mistakes any freelancer can make is being sloppy about security. It's not conducive to a good working relationship if you infect your client's computers with a virus carried on an email you've sent (which is why this topic is mentioned in the CIEP's Code of Practice[6]).

Plan a frequent housekeeping ritual so you can keep your computer well organised and find files easily. And organise your email and folders so that things are readily to hand. This includes planning naming strategies for work files. Some will be dictated by the client, but your working copies need to be well organised so that you know you're working on the right version. Pin files you'll be using a lot to Windows' and/or Word's Quick Access lists – and unpin them when the job is done.

There are people who like to work at a desk with a big computer and there are those who like to work on the sofa with a laptop, which they can also take out into their garden or to the local coffee shop and keep working. Know which you are – but bear in mind that your body may not thank you if you sit hunched up and squinting at a tiny screen trying to mark up a 150,000-word PDF.

Have as big a monitor as you can afford, or will fit on your desk. Many people recommend using two or even three monitors: you can keep reference material open on one and your working document on another. It's perfectly possible to work well with just the one. I use my tablet for reference material as I've not the room for a second monitor, but my 32-inch monitor lets me have two documents open side by side in Word at full size, and has enough room in the tray that I can have many documents and programs open without their thumbnails being stacked.

People who have more than one monitor often recommend having the one with the document they're working on set up portrait style.

Laser printers are fast and cheap and, unless you have a particular need for colour printing, a black-and-white laser multifunction device (prints, photocopies and scans) is a good choice. Double-sided printers are great for saving paper. The ideal of a paperless office is just that – you will probably end up printing things, regardless. Do check out the price of toner cartridges and drums for your shortlist of models before making a final choice.

Broadband speed is critical, especially when using back-up facilities in the cloud, exchanging large files with clients or doing a lot of fact-checking, where slow speeds will be frustrating. If a high-speed service is available in your area and you can afford to do it, I recommend upgrading to the faster speed.

Office environment and furniture

Working at the kitchen table is certainly possible, but not ideal; aim to have a space where you can leave your work undisturbed, and on which you can shut the door at the end of the working day. Have the most comfortable and supportive chair you can afford, a desk you can spread out on and a footrest if you need one (perhaps even one on which you can do exercise). See chapter 6 for more information on **ergonomics and preventing repetitive strain injury (RSI)**.

You'll need somewhere to file finished jobs, at least for a while, and if your work generates paper, this will be more of a physical issue than if everything is backed up in the cloud. Retention time will depend on your client's requirements. Some clients will insist that you delete files and destroy papers as soon as you return the completed work; otherwise, think about keeping jobs until publication, at least. Beyond that, you're now your own boss, so make your space exactly how you want it. If you have green fingers, having plenty of plants will improve air quality.[7] Consider an earthing mat for your feet or your kit if you find you're sensitive to being around a lot of electronics.[8]

Stationery

With your logo file(s) and other branding, you can make your own digital or paper stationery if you need it. Explore the customisable templates in Word and Excel for standard stationery items such as letterheads and invoices, and if you use an accounting package, it will usually have an invoice template that you can customise with your branding. You'll perhaps need an account statement template if your business generates lots of smaller invoices to a client and you need to provide a monthly report of what's been issued, what's been paid and what's outstanding. You may also wish to add your branding to your other business documents, such as a job style sheet or client feedback form. Business cards can be designed very easily and cheaply on the website of one of the many companies offering such services. These days it's probably not necessary to pay a printer for a stack of paper letterheads and invoices, and compliments slips are pretty much redundant, so start small and if you feel the need to have professionally printed stationery (beyond business cards), fine – but don't spend the money until you've established the need. Remember that most business communications are now conducted by email or online. CIEP members should include their CIEP grade-level membership logo[9] on their materials, too, to show prospective clients you're serious about your editing or proofreading.

Reference materials

You will need certain reference materials, depending on the work you plan to do; a shortlist of the most important **reference books** is given in chapter 2, though your own specialism, if you have one, may well dictate additional essential reference works. You should also be aware of the many possible **style guides**, also listed in chapter 2. Different clients may require you to use different dictionaries. Most key resources are available online, often as subscription versions, but for those you use most often, also consider having the paper copy – especially if your internet connection isn't particularly fast.

Website

A website is essential. Even people with an established reputation and lots of network contacts need to advertise sometimes. Potential clients are sure to check you out online and a website gives you a chance to set out your stall, as well as give you a more solid, established feel. See chapter 3 for more about your **website**.

3 | Knowledge

A successful business relies on competent staff (in this case, you), and your profit margin will depend in part on how efficient you are in carrying out the work. It therefore makes sense to be sure that you know your stuff, and to keep up to date. This is recognised by continuing professional development (CPD) being an allowable business expense for income tax purposes. Training to keep you up to date is an allowable business expense; training to enable you to start trading, or to develop a *new* specialism, is not.

Training

Training comes in many forms, but some of the most recognised courses are those provided by the CIEP, the Publishing Training Centre (PTC), Publishing Scotland, Publishing Ireland, the European Association of Science Editors (EASE), the Editorial Freelancers Association (EFA, in the US), Editors Canada and the Institute of Professional Editors (IPEd, in Australia/New Zealand). For members of the CIEP, training is essential to upgrade beyond entry level (or to join as an Intermediate Member or higher); for Advanced Professional Member level, evidence of CPD is required.

If you have had no formal training, even if you have learned on the job but particularly if you are self-taught, do begin with basic proofreading or copyediting skills courses from reputable suppliers, to ensure that you have the nuts and bolts of your trade at your fingertips. Such training will correct any bad habits you may have picked up, fill in gaps in your knowledge you may not even have realised were there, and give confidence to clients that you know what you're doing. Online courses mean you can work at your own pace. In-person workshops will also provide networking and social opportunities.

After you have become solid in the basics, look for training to take your skills to a higher level, including branching out into specialist areas according to your target market or interests. Learn the best techniques for efficient and effective working, advanced Word skills, InDesign, proofreading PDFs, handling references lists, dealing with heavily illustrated books, preparing files as ebooks, editing websites and so on.

No matter how you got your initial training, working on your own means it's far too easy to get absorbed in your own little bubble. CPD is one way you can make sure that you're keeping up with industry standards, keeping your skills fresh rather than relying on the way you've always done it, and engaging with best practice in your profession.

How can I tell what I need to know?

Two of the National Occupational Standards – PUB19 (edit content)[10] and PUB20 (proofread content)[11] – are relevant here. They each give a list of performance criteria for publishing tasks (what you need to be able to do) and of the things you need to know and understand. There's also the syllabus[12] for the CIEP's online editorial test, which gives a pretty good clue about what members are expected to know. Do take note – these lists are of the *least* you should know. They describe the foundation of your knowledge, not the end point.

There is also a CIEP fact sheet on training for copyediting and proofreading, explaining the 'core skills'.[13] Take a look too at the draft Curriculum for Professional Development and the Code of Practice on the CIEP website for other guidance on what you need to know.

CIEP mentoring scheme

You may wish to explore mentoring opportunities, with an experienced copyeditor or proofreader supporting your practice on real materials.[14] Mentoring is available for copyediting and for proofreading. Mentees must have first completed relevant CIEP training courses, or their equivalent, satisfactorily. The mentoring scheme is open to non-members as well as members; CIEP members get a hefty discount on the fee.

Conferences

The annual CIEP conference is well worth going to, no matter how new you are to editing. Attending the conference helps members to feel more part of an actual organisation and to learn direct from each other (and much help is given to first-time attendees to get over the hurdle of meeting real-life fellow editors and proofreaders). You will also benefit from the opportunities to talk to other editorial professionals, share stories, learn new things, have your eyes opened to the things you didn't yet know you didn't know, and to step outside your bubble. And it is invaluable to gain validation for the things you're doing right and to be given a raft of ideas to inspire you.

Other editorial organisations run conferences, too. Those of SENSE (the Dutch English-speaking editors' organisation), METS (Mediterranean Editors and Translators), the Association of Earth Science Editors, the European Association of Science Editors and national editorial associations are popular. Conferences are frequently flagged up on the CIEP member forums, and you can also join the Facebook group Conferences for Editors to find out about more opportunities.

Records

Keep a record of your training and CPD, and use it to work out where the gaps in your knowledge are so you can plan more learning. See chapter 4 on keeping **records**.

Mastering your tools

Almost all editing and proofreading these days is done on screen. There will be exceptions, of course, but the days of sitting quietly with a stack of paper are fading ever more rapidly. This means that copyeditors should be ready to handle Word styles, templates, macros, wildcards and master documents; and, for some jobs, be able to work within clients' systems, which will require you to be computer-savvy and adaptable. The CIEP Macros forum[15] is a great source of help and the other forums are also useful places to ask questions. Proofreaders will need to be competent in marking up PDFs with the tools built in to the program they use, or stamps of the proofreading symbols, according to the client's requirements. The CIEP offers a course on PDF markup.[16]

Be alert, too, to additional software that will improve your efficiency, help cut down on distractions, keep track of your working time, and run your accounts and invoicing (links for many examples of **planning and time management** apps are in chapter 7). CIEP forums, local groups and Facebook groups are great places to ask about and discover the tools that others find useful. Take advantage of free trial periods to road-test different apps to see which work best for you, but do spend some time exploring the features; when you have made your choice, practise using the program so that you get the best out of it for the least effort and therefore increase your efficiency. Time spent doing things the hard way without such tools is time that you could have spent earning money, being with family and friends or just putting your feet up.

Reference books

There are many reference books available, of varying quality and usefulness, and more and more of them have online versions. The online versions can be very handy, but their usefulness pales if your internet connection goes down at a key moment.

The Institute has published a fact sheet for its members on useful reference works when getting started.[17] You will need dictionaries according to the languages and varieties of English you work in. Most publishers will specify the dictionary they want used. Oxford Dictionaries has two levels of access, both powered by the *Oxford English Dictionary* (*OED*), but they are *not* the *OED* and will give you little by way of etymology. Lexico is free and includes a thesaurus. Oxford Dictionaries Premium, for a modest annual fee, gives you access to UK and US dictionaries and thesauruses, as well as a variety of other resources, such as *New Hart's Rules* (*NHR*), the *New Oxford Dictionary for Writers & Editors* (*NODWE*), *Garner's Dictionary of Legal Usage* and *Pocket Fowler's Modern English Usage*, but *not* the *Oxford English Dictionary* (*OED*).

But give serious consideration to also owning physical versions of those you find you use most – probably *NHR* and *NODWE*. The *New Oxford Spelling Dictionary* (*NOSD*) and Oxford Dictionaries Premium are particularly useful for proofreaders as they show where word breaks should fall.

The annual subscription to the online version of the *full OED* is eye-watering for a freelancer, but an individual subscription to Oxford Dictionaries Premium should suffice for most tasks. If you're in the UK, also check out what your library offers. Many local libraries will give you access to lots of Oxford and other resources free of charge and you can log in to their websites using your library card number. The libraries page of your council's website may well list the resources available this way.

You may want your own copy of other books, including *Butcher's Copy-Editing* (now in its 4th edition) and *Fowler's Dictionary of Modern English Usage*. *The Chicago Manual of Style* (*CMoS*, also online) is a mainstay for many who edit in US English, together with *Garner's Modern English Usage* (newly retitled from *Garner's Modern American Usage*).

You may well have subject specialisms that need reference works, too. As you add to your collection, anything you buy through Amazon will give the CIEP a small commission (from Amazon's pocket, not yours), if you use a special link to begin your purchases.[18] Look at the CIEP website for reviews of new books in the editorial and language fields.

Check the Benefits section in the members' area of the CIEP website to see what discounts are available.

Style guides

It is informative and eye-opening to consider some of the many style guides commercially available. There is a (small) selection at the Wikipedia page on style guides[19] that you might explore, especially if your previous experience has been rather narrow.

And, of course, each publisher (and enlightened companies and organisations) will have their own style guide, such as the BBC,[20] the UK government[21] and BuzzFeed,[22] which is interesting for its capture of current buzzwords. *Simplified Technical English*[23] is invaluable for those who edit in that field, as is *Scientific Style and Format*.[24]

Not all clients have a style guide. If you have to work one out for a job, Christina Thomas and Abi Saffrey's CIEP guide *Your House Style: Styling your words for maximum impact*[25] has lots of helpful advice on what should be included in a house style. It also lists useful guidelines for websites and print material.

Social media and online communities

This is the time to embrace social media and online communities, if you've been holding back. They are an invaluable resource for getting advice, problem-solving and picking up tips on best practice, and ultimately for marketing your business. You do not need to be active on every social media platform, but it will quickly ground you in editorial conversations if you pick one that suits you. The CIEP forums are the first port of call for members.[26] Being part of our vibrant community is a huge benefit of membership. The forums cover general practice issues, newbies, macros and a marketplace to find work passed on by other members, plus forums for each local group and the Cloud Clubs, and specialist areas such as fiction, ELT (English language teaching), education, legal, MedSTEM (science/technical/engineering/medical, focusing on medical editing) and more.

> Join the forums and your CIEP local group if you have one. It's enormously helpful when you're just getting going to realise that you're not on your own, and you can get lots of great support and advice from colleagues – some of whom are in the same position as you, while others have been in the same position in the past.

Steve Hammatt

The Institute also has official accounts and pages on Facebook, LinkedIn and Twitter, providing curated content of interest to editors and proofreaders, and announcements of new resources – such as fact sheets and blogs.

Facebook groups such as the Editors' Association of Earth (EAE)[27] and its associated subgroups (especially EAE Backroom), as well as The Unofficial CIEP[28] are also fantastic places to check usage with native speakers of different Englishes. It's rare that you will work just in UK English, so if you want to see whether a phrase works in another English, these groups are great places to get a quick, informed response (but do be prepared for huge regional difference in usage, within any given country). There are many editors' and proofreaders' groups on Facebook and LinkedIn, but do tread carefully and judge which ones are populated with people who will steer you in the right direction. When joining Facebook groups, check out the files tab – both EAE and Business + Professional Development for Editors in particular have some great resources there, and they're too often overlooked.

Consider keeping your personal and professional presences online distinct. You may well want to create a Facebook page for your business and keep clients there, and have a separate Twitter account. If your online presence has been less than professional, you may also want to think about culling posts so that you present only a professional aspect

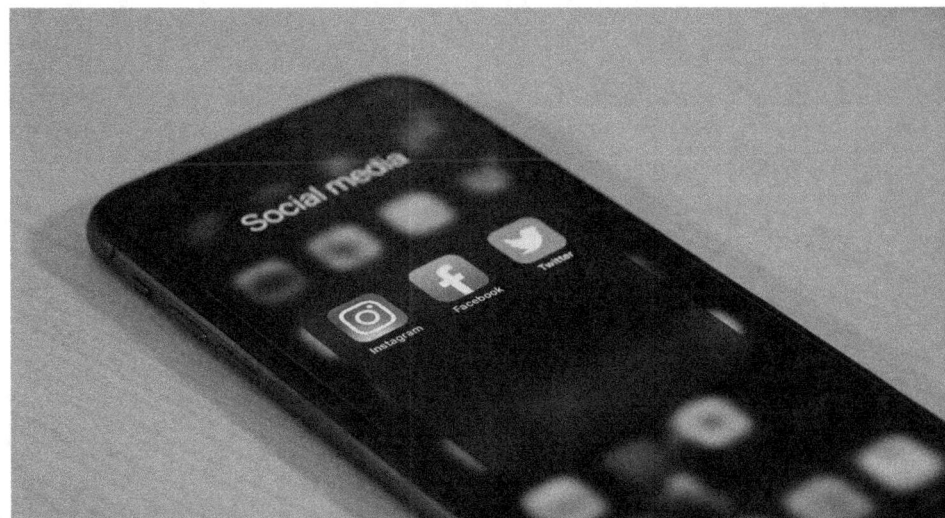

to potential clients. On Twitter, do get to grips with lists to organise your editorial followings into a coherent thread, rather than lose them in the midst of all the other noise.

If you are very new, joining groups on Facebook and/or LinkedIn or following people and organisations on Twitter can be educational, even if you only lurk (read posts without writing any of your own). And even lurking will help keep you aware of current events in the editorial world – avoiding that comfortable little bubble.

If you cannot abide the thought of Facebook, then give the Editors Lair website a go – it was deliberately set up as a non-Facebook editorial group of like-minded folk.[29] There's nothing to stop you joining both for maximum coverage!

Continuing professional development

The world of publishing, and the production of documents in other fields, is changing faster and faster. New tools and new norms are developing all the time. Think about your CPD to ensure that you do not get left behind, and can stay competitive in what you are able to offer to your clients. When preparing your budgets, be sure to allocate some expenditure to CPD each year.

Less formal CPD can involve keeping abreast of publishing news, via channels such as *The Bookseller*[30] and the Publishing Perspectives website,[31] reading books and blogs related to your practice and interests, and participating in the CIEP forums and local groups.[32] The Copyeditors' Knowledge Base[33] by Katharine O'Moore-Klopf is a great source of ideas for reading and CPD, as well as answering knotty questions.

In any event you will want to keep up to date with language change – the new, welcome focus on diversity is raising all manner of issues for editorial professionals, and you will need to be in a position to guide your clients, if need be. The Conscious Style Guide[34] will be a real help.

4 | Clients

Finding work

This is probably the single most daunting aspect of going solo. No one can guarantee you work. You must go out and find it; where you pitch yourself will depend on your chosen niche. If you already have any contacts at all in the area you want to work in (former employer, friend-of-a-friend), use them.

The Institute has a short fact sheet on finding your first clients.[35]

And while this may seem a harsh thing to say to someone just starting out, it's worthwhile remembering this from the get-go: do *not* become reliant on a small number of clients. The comfort and security of regular jobs can make you cut back prematurely on your marketing efforts, and if that client no longer comes to you (whether they start using someone else, or go out of business, or there's a pandemic that disrupts things around the world) then you could be left painfully in the lurch.

Cold-emailing

If you want to work for publishers, a good starting point is the *Writers' and Artists' Yearbook* (either a physical copy or the online version[36]), which contains listings of UK publishers, what they publish and their contact information. Search through, marking those publishers you intend to approach. Contact the switchboard to get the name and job title of the person responsible for editorial freelancers; write or email, including your CV tailored towards that particular client (stressing relevant experience or knowledge useful to that client).

Packagers, or prepress companies, take on that part of the job between the publisher deciding that the book is to be published and printing the finished copies – copyediting, typesetting, redrawing artwork, proofreading and indexing. They can be a good way in to working on good-quality books. Check our fact sheet on working with packagers for advice on what to consider.[37]

Try searching **Yell.com** under 'Publishers', 'Book Publishers', 'Prepress Services', 'Printers and Lithographers', 'Newspapers and Magazines' or any other search term you think likely, to discover companies who may be in a position to offer work.

Don't phone (cold-calling) – you don't know that the person has time to talk to you there and then; they may well not note down your information, and they'll have nothing to refer to later. One thing you can say of all publishers is that they're very busy and they don't want their day sent off track by cold-callers.

> *Keep plugging away at those enquiries to potential clients (keeping a record of approaches and responses) and do any proofreading/copyediting test going.*
>
> Krysia Johnson

If you want to work with businesses, take a similar approach. Browse online for businesses that you're interested in, and find out who to contact.

> *Target those who publish (be it publishers, self-publishers, companies, and so on) in your area of expertise, be it geography, knitting, law or computer programming. Potential clients are far more likely to want to take a chance with a newbie with area expertise than with one without. And make sure you keep a careful list of those you contact, and follow up each communication.*
>
> Janet MacMillan

If your interest is in academic journals, you need to contact the publishers of the journals, again searching online.

In all cases, do take the trouble to find out exactly whom you should approach – if you can't find out via websites, phone the organisation and ask. And then make sure you spell the person's name and job title correctly.

CIEP members can join the Marketplace forum, where other members post job offers they can't take on, and there is also the Editors' Association of Earth's (EAE) Ad Space on Facebook, where job offers are posted, and people can say that they're looking for work.

Note that for the purposes of upgrading to Professional Member and beyond, you will need experience of working for organisations that are in a position to recognise good and bad editing or proofreading when they see it, such as traditional book publishers. If you don't work for such clients, you can take the CIEP's online editorial test – passing that will show that you do know your stuff, even if your clients won't necessarily be sufficiently involved in the editorial world themselves to judge properly. This is something to keep in mind if you work for individual authors or self-publishing companies – those who provide publishing services to authors for a fee, regardless of the quality of the book. Some of these companies doubtless have excellent quality control. Others definitely don't, and as it is impossible for the CIEP to keep abreast of where any given company is on the continuum of quality, if you work only or mainly for such companies you will need a test pass to upgrade.

Offshoring

Be aware that many UK publishers now have their prepress services offshored, which is to say that they are project-managed overseas, from copyediting all the way through to producing files ready to print, quite often in the enormous publishing industry in India. Many of these jobs will specify an editor whose dominant language is the English of the book's target market. Many of the jobs will also have been through a pre-editing process where, in effect, the typesetter gets a jump-start on coding the text ready for typesetting before it's been edited. Coping with such files is a skill in itself – and an important one. This offshoring has had mixed success. Given that the purpose was to get this part of book production completed more cheaply, fees are suitably depressed, and editors may well not get the support they need when asking even straightforward questions about the job. On the other hand, many CIEP members make this their bread-and-butter work and find the companies they work for perfectly fine. As with all prospective clients, go in with your eyes open and check the forums for feedback and discussion.

Working for students

Many beginning editors consider working with students on theses and dissertations as a way of building up experience and getting an income. While this is a lively market, be aware that there are ethical considerations and in fact it may take more skill and judgement to do this sort of work. Each educational institution will have rules regarding what help a student may receive – references sections, for example, may be out of bounds – and you should ensure that the student is allowed to seek editorial help, and find out to what extent you may go in the edit. Stephen Cashmore's CIEP guide *Proofreading Theses and Dissertations*[38] includes a discussion on setting parameters for your work and arranging payment.

Marketing and advertising

You can also advertise and wait for the work to come to you. Professional and Advanced Professional Members of the CIEP can take out an entry in the CIEP Directory;[39] Intermediate Members can list themselves in IM Available.[40] If you've completed certain PTC courses, you can take out an entry in its Freelance Finder listings.[41]

Thomson Local, Yell, FreeIndex and other online directories offer free entries, as does Google My Business. Or you can buy a paid entry in Yell, for example, which you can personalise with keywords and a description of your services, and which will link to your website. Check to see whether your local authority runs a business directory.

Sara Hulse's CIEP guide *Marketing Yourself: Strategies to promote your editorial business* contains many cost-effective marketing ideas, as does Louise Harnby's *Marketing Your Editing & Proofreading Business* (see **Resources** section).

Online companies offering all kinds of editing and proofreading are proliferating, most emphasising an incredibly fast turnaround time and zero 'errors' in the material after it's been worked on. Aside from the pressures that puts on the editorial professionals, it also raises unrealistic expectations; we all know that there are many ways English can be used to express an idea, that spelling is, in some cases, a preference and that the correct use of the comma, the semicolon and so on is a matter of opinion and what you're used to. The CIEP has guidance on standards in proofreading[42] and acceptable error rates. Still, if you need to get a foot in the door, you could investigate these and sign up with directories and agencies. Be wary of the ones that expect money from you up front. They should be making their profit in the margin between what they charge the customer and what they pay you. Some are perfectly reputable, though. Do your homework, and you may find this a fruitful route to work (and enhanced SEO). CIEP members would be well advised to search the forums for opinions before signing up with any agency. Many are a race to the bottom and highly competitive. I've seen evidence of people earning less than a pound an hour through some of these agencies. That is *not* a sustainable business model for you. Far better to spend your time searching for decent clients than earning that kind of money.

Should you work for nothing, or for peanuts, just to get going?

When you're desperate for a job – any job – so you can start building a portfolio, gathering testimonials and adding to your CV, it's tempting to work for nothing (or 'for the exposure' as some optimistic would-be clients put it). By all means volunteer your time to an organisation close to your heart, but think extremely carefully about doing unpaid work. What does that tell the client about how you value the service you offer? How will you manage the swap to paid work for that client in future? What value will there be in a testimonial from a client who is not in a position to know whether you've done the job to professional standards?

A quid pro quo, however, is quite different. Be sure the exchange is something of real value to you so you don't feel that you're being taken advantage of – and note that its cash equivalent will still be counted as taxable income (see chapter 5 for more on **income tax, National Insurance and VAT**). Perhaps you can proofread something for someone who can be your business guru, editing teacher or informal mentor, or can help build your website.

Website

Your website will be as useful as you make it. Many clients will expect some sort of web presence from their potential editors and proofreaders, and it's usual for potential clients to check you out online. You can have a website built for you, but it is increasingly easy to build your own using WordPress (**wordpress.com**) or Weebly (**weebly.com**), for example. Search "build your own website" online (use double quote marks to search the exact phrase) for many more providers.[43]

> *Personally I found that getting a website and getting it 'visible' online made a huge difference.*
>
> Myriam Birch

If you register your own domain name,[44] you can have businesslike email addresses that enhance your professional appearance, rather than one from your internet service provider (ISP) or Gmail, say.

Include a clear description of what problems you can solve for your clients (all the more so if you are targeting clients who may not understand traditional editorial services, such as businesses), what services you offer and how you can be contacted. You should explain your cookie policy and your privacy policy,[45] and be sure you comply with the General Data Protection Regulation (GDPR).[46] Take care to optimise your website's findability with good SEO word choices, but don't use 'keyword stuffing' as search engines' algorithms may penalise you by dropping you down the results.

FutureLearn offers a two-week course (two hours per week) by Accenture on digital marketing, including SEO, which runs every few weeks, as at the time of writing.[47] More advanced and involved courses are also available, including about social media – just search FutureLearn for "digital skills" (again, use double quote marks to search the exact phrase).

Consider adding a blog, if you think you have plenty to say on editorial matters, but be aware that you need to post regularly, if not frequently, as a clearly unattended blog sends out the wrong message. And don't overlook **content marketing** – see chapter 1.

Adapting your CV

One size does *not* fit all when it comes to CVs. Keep it short. Two pages, good; one page, better. If you can't fit it all on one page, keep the most salient information on the front page – contact details, services offered, recent experience. Save effort by having a core CV that you then adapt for each client you send it to. Keep it classy, and lay it out clearly. This is your shopfront and you want to demonstrate to the client that you are up to the job. If you are sending your CV to a business, highlight your experience and knowledge of business matters and editing, and don't use up a paragraph on your fiction-editing experience. If you're sending it to a fiction publisher, don't have your non-fiction editing foremost.

Don't include any personal information unless it is *directly* relevant to your client. A keen sailor would want to mention that to a publisher of sailing books, for instance, whereas your fostering of children or of kittens would be relevant to different clients.

If you are sending your CV in hard copy, pop a business card in the envelope, too, loose, so that the recipient has two chances of finding your contact details if, as is quite probable, they keep business cards separate from their filing of A4 paper.

Keep your covering letter, or covering email, short and to the point. Introduce yourself, and say why you're approaching that potential client. Suggest why you're a good match for them, and refer them to your accompanying CV for further information.

Networking

Networking is essential for your business at some level. If you are looking to work for businesses, you may find it useful to join your local chamber of commerce[48] and go to events, armed with your business cards and elevator pitch (see next subsection).

Use social media – some people find work directly this way. Others use it as an additional way of making their presence known, so that potential clients can look for them and gain reassurance that they are a genuine, viable business and a knowledgeable individual. The most business-focused site is LinkedIn, which can serve as an online CV. Facebook and Twitter are also popular. Follow the organisations that form your target market, and engage in dialogue with them. Instagram and Reddit are also gaining inroads into the editorial arena.

BookMachine[49] runs all kinds of networking events for the publishing world online and in person, and the CIEP occasionally partners with them.

> *Don't burn bridges, no matter how much that may seem justified when leaving an in-house job, voluntarily or otherwise. I recently completed a six-week contract, with the promise of more work to come, for the chap who made me redundant six years ago.*
>
> Steve Garnsey

If you want to work with self-publishing authors, there are many writers' groups and networking websites, and agencies that aim to put editor/proofreader and author together. Take a look at the Society of Authors[50] and ALLi, the Alliance of Independent Authors,[51] to start with – but there are many such organisations.

Elevator pitches

The term 'elevator pitch' is taken from how much you can say to win a new client in the length of time it takes to go up in the lift with them. Elevator pitches are great to have ready for in-person networking.[52] Practise explaining in soundbites why someone should hire you. Do it in front of a mirror until you can sell yourself and your business succinctly, at the drop of a hat.

Working with your clients

Pricing the work

The CIEP publishes suggested minimum rates per hour for proofreading, copyediting, substantive editing/rewriting/development editing, project management and indexing.[53] Discussions among editorial professionals, though, show the wide range of fees actually paid. It is clear there is no 'going rate' for editorial work in the UK or elsewhere.

Melanie Thompson's CIEP guide *Pricing a Project: How to prepare a professional quotation*[54] is full of excellent advice on how to work out what to charge in far greater breadth and detail than can be included here. Maintaining detailed records of the work you do will set you on the road to your own database that will help you calculate time and money estimates for new jobs (see what **experience** you need to record in chapter 4).

Remember that your fee must cover your time (working and admin time) and your outgoings, and leave you with a profit. That said, pricing yourself out of the market won't help.

The *An American Editor* blog frequently has articles on pricing and other editorial business matters.[55] It usually talks in terms of price per page (a predominantly American measure – a 'page' for pricing purposes is considered to be 250 words), but even if you charge another way it does make you think about ensuring your price structure will make a living for you.

> *If you want to pitch for higher fees, make sure your quotation gives enough information to show what good value your services are. Don't assume clients want the cheapest price.*
>
> John Firth

Negotiating price and timescale

Increasingly, publishers and prepress services providers (aka packagers) quote a fixed price for the job. Whether that price is what you want it to be is, of course, debatable and will vary from job to job and person to person.

Review the materials for the job as soon as they arrive, and check that you have everything. Then look through them and form a view on whether it's possible to do that job in the time allowed and for the fee offered. If you won't get the materials until the job is due to start, you'll have to assess whether the fee and timescale sound reasonable from your experience of other jobs and the information your client gives you, but then do review this as soon as the job arrives.

If you consider that the fee or timescale is inadequate, you will need to go back to the client and state your case, negotiating for more time and/or money. Here is where your growing database of jobs done and time taken against fee earned will be invaluable. You are a business, and you must take a businesslike approach to this, or you will find yourself working long, unsocial hours for peanuts and growing an ulcer, neither of which you bargained for when you decided to work for yourself.

If, on the other hand, you're asked to name your price, you will need to have in mind the bare minimum below which you will not go – the figure at which it would be a better use of your time to forgo this job and market yourself elsewhere. Also have in mind the price you would love to be paid for the job and start at that figure. If you can, get the client to state their budget first: you may be pleasantly surprised and thus paid better than you'd dare hope; or you may realise that there is no way you will come to terms, and save yourself the time and energy of negotiating on a job you cannot afford to take.

If you're asked to state how much time you need, programme in some wiggle room. How much will depend on the scale of the job, but your estimate of the date you will return the job to the client is *not* from how many hours the job itself will take, but how much time will elapse before it's completed. If you have commitments with your family, or another job, or you want to finish early one day, an eight-hour job may be finished in three days or a week. An 80-hour job may be finished in a month or six weeks. Or longer, or shorter, depending on what else is going on in your life. The larger the job, the more wiggle room you'll need to include.

Scheduling the work

There are many elements to scheduling, but the three main ones are:

- How many hours of work are needed for the job?
- What else am I doing at the same time?
- How much work can I do per day before my head explodes and quality goes down the drain?

Never, ever, *plan* to work at 100% capacity. What will you do if there is any kind of glitch? You get a tummy bug, the work is more involved than you thought, there's a storm and your power is cut? And if you routinely give 100%, what will you do when more is demanded? That way lie ill-health and meltdowns.

As a rule of thumb, you're unlikely to be effective for more than five hours of editing or proofreading per day. After that, fatigue will probably set in and your concentration will walk out of the door. If five hours seems short, note that it's considered that five hours' productivity is all that office-based employees can give each day, once you factor in time lost to conversations, meetings, phone calls, company (rather than task) emails and so on. I've seen some studies that think it's more like three hours, and one that says it's six hours, but only if you take good breaks.

> *Time is a really important resource. If you choose to accept a slightly lower rate for a certain job, not having a lot of time pressure is really helpful so you can fit it around better paid work that may be more urgent.*

Andrew Hodges

Aside from time working on editorial tasks, you will be marketing and networking, keeping your accounts up to date, reviewing your business and laying new plans and goals, undertaking CPD, and seeking ways to work more efficiently and to make your business more robust. All of these take time, and all of them are the first things to be jettisoned if you try to fit too much editing or proofreading into your day. Yet as a business owner, you need to do *all* of this stuff yourself, now.

How you schedule depends on how you like to see your life set out, and whether you work on lots of short jobs with tight deadlines, or bigger jobs with longer deadlines and more wiggle room. You'll need some kind of scheduling help – a diary with *all* your commitments in it, whether online or on paper.

I usually work on book-length jobs, so clients' schedules are generally a month, ish. I have clients booked loosely into slots a few months ahead. Each year I print a free A4 planner.[56] I mark each firmly scheduled job with a line of highlighter from the start date to the due date, which I label with the client and job name by writing along the highlighter line, and I literally pencil in those roughly reserved slots so I can see whom I need to inform as the start date becomes more defined, as well as whether I can take on an urgent, shorter job. This won't work for everyone, especially if you schedule in several jobs per day because you work on short articles, marketing pieces or the like. In that case, an online diary would work much better – such as Outlook's schedule (or whatever came with your email program), Calendar (Apple's calendar), Google Calendar, Toggl Plan and many others.

> *Don't be afraid to say no to jobs. If you don't think you have time to do it, you won't. If you don't want to do it, don't. Whether you say yes or no, they may, or may not, ask you to work with them again. But if you say yes and do a poor job, it's unlikely they will ask you again.*

Julia Sandford-Cooke

Sample edits and tests for prospective clients

If a publisher wants you to take a test to get into their freelancer pool, take the test – but if it's a stupidly long test, you may not think it worth your while. After all, you're working for nothing while you're doing the test. Weigh up the pros and cons of taking a long test before completing it. It's also possible that after a changeover of staff in a publisher, the new people will want all their freelancers to take a new test so that they can judge how people edit, and see what strengths and weaknesses individuals have. If you like the client, don't be offended – take the new test. It's not necessarily a Bad Thing! It gives you a chance to show them what you can do. This happened to me less than a year ago, and resulted in three back-to-back books being scheduled right away.

If an indie client (a business client or an individual) wants to see a sample edit, again, think about it first. Some editorial professionals make a point of offering a free sample on the grounds that it helps you gauge the amount of intervention the job needs, and it helps the client gauge whether you're the right editor or proofreader for them. There have, however, been instances of entrepreneurial individuals trying to get a different editor to edit every chapter in their book as a 'free sample', scoring what they see as a free edit (aka a Frankenedit) and what we know will be an appalling mishmash. Again, trust your instincts. Use the CIEP forums to see if anyone else has been approached. Do not, however, show a prospective client before-and-after documents from other clients. That is a clear breach of confidentiality.

If you want to offer free samples, be clear on how many words you will edit or proofread, and ask for a sample from the middle of the work; some would say ask for bits from the start, middle and end. It's probable that the first chapter or two of a book will have been worked on far more than the rest of the text.

An alternative is to offer paid samples – and then offset the price of the sample from the final invoice if you are given the job, so the client doesn't get charged twice for the extent of the sample. This also tests the water for communication and the client's approach to actually paying for work.

CIEP Code of Practice and client relations

The CIEP Code of Practice[57] is a source of excellent best-practice advice on the ethical running of your business and, by joining the Institute, members agree to abide by it. There are additional documents available on the CIEP website advising freelancers and clients on how to deal with each other.[58,59]

Contracts and terms and conditions

Some company clients will have a contract they will issue to you, setting out the responsibilities of both parties, you and the client. It's as well, though, to have your own set of terms and conditions (T&Cs) ready that you can issue to clients in the absence of a contract (for instance, when working with individual authors). The CIEP has model T&Cs[60] in the members' area, which may save you a lot of work in figuring out what to include.

Many publishers and prepress companies don't ask for a separate contract or signed T&Cs – an exchange of emails offering and accepting the work is binding. Increasingly, however, publishers require a contract (either one per job, or one that covers all jobs). Be aware that some of these standard contracts carelessly retain some clauses intended for corporate suppliers, or suppliers of very different services, that really don't apply to editorial freelancers or that put unfair burdens on them. So read carefully any contract you are offered, and query or challenge any clauses that seem onerous – such as demanding indemnification for any losses, perhaps without an upper limit, or restricting for whom else you can work. It may take some determination to get the offending clause(s) struck out, but it is achievable much of the time.

Give careful thought to going ahead with the job without a signed contract, though, in case things get sticky, and don't leave yourself exposed to working for nothing. Yet again, the CIEP forums are a good place to check how other people have handled a boilerplate contract from any given publisher. In addition, Professional and Advanced Professional Members of the CIEP can consult the legal helpline[61] regarding contracts they're unsure about.

T&Cs and contracts should protect both parties, spelling out what the work is, when it is due, what the fee is and when it will be paid, and what happens if something goes wrong, on either side.

> *Think about your professional boundaries ahead of time, and work these into a terms and conditions document your clients must read and agree to. This will save you from headaches regarding details around deposits, cancellations, scope creep and much more.*
>
> Sophie Playle

If you work with individuals – such as authors or other small businesses – have your own T&Cs worked out and get the client to sign and return a copy. For individual clients, especially first-time clients, you may wish to request part (or all) of the payment up front, with the rest payable before or on delivery of the edited/proofread work. This information must be in your T&Cs.

Karin Cather and Dick Margulis, stalwarts of EAE, have produced the excellent *The Paper It's Written On*,[62] which breaks down all the topics your T&Cs need to cover and looks at scenarios where a well-written contract could have saved a great deal of trouble. Although both authors are American, the principles are applicable globally.

Red flags and firing clients

Some job offers may make you nervous. When you're trying to establish yourself in your new business, it's tempting to ignore those feelings and take the job and the money. But if you do, you may get more than you bargained for – a nightmare client, a nightmare schedule or an unpaid invoice. Trust your instincts. Some jobs are more trouble than they're worth.

One of the joys of freelancing is that you get to pick and choose your clients. If you don't want to work with someone, you don't have to. You can just say no. I see some editorial freelancers tie themselves in knots giving reasons for turning the work down without hurting the client's feelings, or trying to fix the client up with another editor or proofreader. I've found the simplest approach is to say, as I did to one recent potential client, 'Thank you for contacting me, but I won't be quoting for this work. I wish you well in your search for an appropriate editor to work with. Many thanks for considering me.' If I think the client may be worth pursuing, even though I can't take on the job myself, I point them to the CIEP Directory. If I detect red flags, I'll not try to find an editor for them at all – it's not kind to dump that person on someone else and make it their problem!

If you've taken on a client, and things go sour – perhaps they consistently pay late, so you have to chase up every invoice, perhaps they send promised work late but won't move the deadline for return of the files, perhaps they have a new project manager you don't get on with – you can fire them. The next time they want to send you work, say no (if you want to leave the door open to future offers, just say that your schedule is full), and go and find a client you like better. You don't have to do business with people you don't want to do business with. You're in charge of that.

> *It's important to not be afraid to say no. If the schedule isn't right, if the price isn't right, or if your gut just says 'I don't like this', it's best to say no. Something better almost always comes along instead, and it's better to spend time on marketing/ websites/networking and so on than to work for pennies on a project that has you tearing your hair out and questioning what you've done with your life!*

Kate Haigh

Lisa Cordaro has written a pair of blog posts about how to stay safe, in a business sense, as an editorial freelancer.[63]

If things are so bad you need to fire the client in the middle of the job, then a well-crafted set of T&Cs or contract will save the day.

If you do fire a client, don't be surprised if you feel pretty weird about it and keep worrying whether you've done the right thing. A trawl through editorial social media will show that this is a common reaction, and you'll see a whole host of fellow editors and proofreaders reassuring people that ditching a toxic client is a wise move.

5 | Records

The first rule of knowing what records to keep is: work out what you want to get *from* your records.

Records can be:

- statutory (for tax purposes)
- tools (for estimating purposes or to support an upgrade application)
- business stats that will inform decisions of many kinds.

Statutory records

A reminder: the specifics here relate to the UK, so research your own requirements if you live elsewhere. HMRC requires that you record all your income and business expenses, where the money came from and where it went, in order to calculate your profits and thus your tax and National Insurance.[64] You are entitled to claim the costs of working from home, and you will need to record the number of hours actually spent working, in order to make the necessary calculations (which can include all the time spent working for the business, so on admin, marketing and CPD, for example, as well as actually editing and proofreading) each and every day.

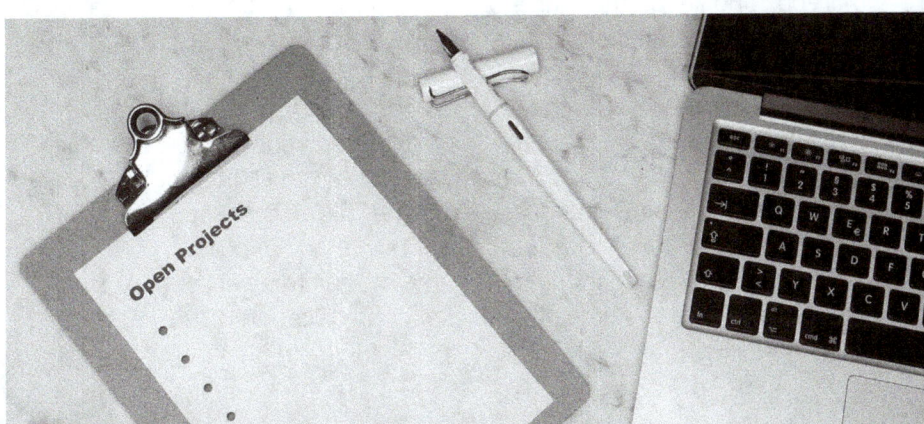

Record-keeping is a legal requirement. You will need to keep careful and accurate records of who has paid you, how much, what for and when. You will need to keep equally accurate and careful records of what you have spent, when you spent it, what you spent it on and whether it was an allowable business or capital expense for tax relief purposes.

For your own sanity, it is best to keep these records as you go along. This will enable you to complete your tax return promptly, help to prevent receipts and invoices going astray, and ensure you will be ready and able to comply with Making Tax Digital (MTD), coming in April 2023. MTD will mean you must keep your records in a way such that they can be uploaded to the HMRC website for tax assessment purposes. In the meantime, you can keep your records on paper, in a spreadsheet, or in proprietary software ready to 'bridge' to the MTD service. You must keep these records securely, and for the period specified by HMRC. If your house burns down or is flooded, or your computer blows up, you will still be expected to produce your records to complete your tax return (or should you be subject to an HMRC audit), and excuses are not accepted. You will be required to reconstruct your records, even if that means paying to get copies of statements and receipts.

This means, in brief, scanning or photographing your receipts (including the back, if there's anything written on it), backing up your accounts files in multiple places and perhaps investing in a firebox[65] to protect precious paper originals – any document relating to tax paid *must* be kept as a paper original (P45s, P60s, payslips, taxed interest bank statements and so on) although all other documentation is fine as an image only. I have a firebox and keep other hard-to-replace items in it, too. It's *not* a safe, but it is intended to protect the contents against high temperatures. If you scan anything, check the quality of the image before ditching the paper copy (by all means scan the tax documentation as back-up, but *don't* ditch the paper copy). Keep backups onsite and somewhere else, such as in the cloud. If your records are lost, do inform HMRC right away, and start reconstructing your accounts sooner rather than later.

Now would be a good time to look into moving to an accounting system. FreeAgent is, at the time of writing, offering discounted subscriptions to

CIEP members.⁶⁶ It enables you to photograph your receipts, submit your tax return and link through to your business bank account. Some editors use other similar platforms, such as QuickBooks and QuickFile. HMRC is encouraging people to join its pilot scheme for MTD, and a digital accounting system is one prerequisite. Starting early also lets you change system if the first one you pick doesn't suit you, *before* MTD is live.

Personally, I run my accounts on spreadsheets, for now. How you organise your own records will depend on what fits with the way you think, and how far along you are with moving over to one of the bridging apps in preparation for MTD. I fully expect my own record-keeping to change over the coming years.

You must keep all your financial records until five years after the last filing date for any given year.⁶⁷

The last filing date is 31 January after the end of the tax year, so records for the 2020/21 tax year must be kept until at least 31 January 2027 (last filing date for 2020/21 is 31 January 2022 plus five years). Check the **Going Solo Toolkit** if you're a CIEP member to see if MTD changes this. Financial records include not just copies of receipts and invoices, but anything relating to money coming in and out of your business, and income from other sources: bank statements, credit card statements, paying-in and cheque stubs and any records of tax paid, such as P45s, P60s, and tax paid on pensions, interest and benefits and any other income.

Other essential records

Experience

You'll need to record key facts about each job you do. These will enable you to keep track of when invoices are due to be paid and whether they have been, and to build up a store of data from which you can calculate increasingly accurate estimates for new jobs.

The CIEP guide *Pricing a Project* contains more information on what records to keep. A basic free template spreadsheet is available,[68] which you can customise to suit your own business, that shows the wealth of data you can collect on jobs undertaken to help you with estimating the price and cost of new jobs.

> *Keep a detailed spreadsheet of jobs: type of work, fee, number of words, rate in words per hour, hourly paid rate. Use this when giving quotes for new jobs and for identifying clients who pay well or badly.*
>
> Hester Higton

For upgrading, you'll need to record the hours (not days, not weeks) spent on each job, how much of it was in the core skills (copyediting and/or proofreading, *not* translating, indexing, teaching English or creating new content, though a small proportion of development editing and/or project management can be included in your experience, if necessary), who the client was and when the job was carried out. This information will also help you understand how your business is developing.

Training and CPD

To plan your training budget, and for upgrading, you'll need to keep a training log. Ensure that enough of your training is in the core skills, and that you have sufficient CPD, according to the grade you're applying for. Seeing your training laid out in one place will make the identification of skills gaps easier, in conjunction with your thoughts on how you want to develop your business. You may also want to display your training in your Directory entry (Professional Members and above).

> *Record your CPD – even the informal stuff – from the outset. It doesn't much matter how, as long as you do it. It's so much easier to complete an upgrade application if you have it all at your fingertips.*
>
> Jane Moody

CIEP members can download a template spreadsheet in the **Going Solo Toolkit** to record your training history, and to keep track of your training plans. It helps you to break down your training into core skills (copyediting and proofreading) and other training, in preparation for upgrading.[69]

Desirable records

For marketing purposes, you'll want to know where your clients are finding you – advertising, job-finding websites, your own website through an internet search, personal recommendation, cold-emailing and so on – so do remember to find out, and to record, where approaches are coming from and for which service, whether you take on the job or not.

Keep records of your active marketing – who have you contacted, what was the response, when did you follow up?

You will also want to be able to analyse the data you've collected to find out which clients pay best, which kind of work pays best, and which clients pay worst, or always need chasing. Some people have a policy of firing their lowest-paying or most irritating client each year – it may take you a while to have the capacity to do that, but it's a good policy to pursue. You can also see whether you're getting faster, especially if you start using a new efficiency tool such as PerfectIt or macros, or after taking a course.

CIEP Advanced Professional Member Sophie Playle blogs each year on her review of her business records and turns that into new goals for the forthcoming year; she also provides a workbook so you can follow her process.[70]

Maya Berger, also a CIEP Advanced Professional Member, has brought all the different kinds of records into a single system: The Editor's Affairs (TEA).[71]

6 | Money

The importance of keeping track

Financial records fulfil very important functions. First, of course, you *must* comply with the requirements to keep track of income and expenditure for income tax and National Insurance contributions (NICs) purposes (see 'Statutory records' in chapter 4). But beyond that, your records will tell you whether you're profitable and are charging enough, and whether clients have paid their invoices or you need to chase them up, and will provide an invaluable resource when it comes to pricing work – see chapter 4.

What does your income need to cover?

In addition to the outgoings you always had as an employee (food, housing, council tax, clothing, insurance, heating, lighting, entertainment, transport, pet care ...), your self-employment earnings have to cover:

- tax
- National Insurance
- pension
- training costs
- office consumables and equipment
- memberships and subscriptions
- networking costs
- marketing materials
- heating and lighting for longer if you work from home
- office or co-working space costs if you don't work from home
- 'sick pay'
- 'holiday pay'
- a cushion to keep you going if your cash flow hits a problem.

Think whether there's anything you need to add to this list that is a 'new' expense as a freelancer.

Instead of income tax, NICs and pension[72,73] payments being taken at source by your employer, you will now need to budget for these (see the **Going Solo Toolkit** for more on pensions). You will also want to make provision for times you can't or don't want to work by saving for the equivalent of sick or holiday pay.

By drawing up a full budget that covers *all* your outgoings, you will discover how much you need to earn, in terms of how much work you do and how much per hour you need to charge. If you commuted and will now be working at home, there's at least one saving. If you needed smart office wear, you may find you need to spend less on clothing. You will now, though, need to heat and light your home all day or pay the costs of your own working space. Your figures will necessarily be estimates for several items at this stage. Put in your most pessimistic figures. There's no point in going solo if it means financial ruin for you.

What follows is based on straightforward circumstances in the UK. If yours aren't – you have other sources of income, you have employees or you are outside the UK – you should seek advice from HMRC direct[74] (or your country's tax authority, as appropriate), or from an accountant.

Income tax, National Insurance and VAT

Your approach to your business is up to you. Whether it's something you do on the side for a little extra cash or to build up a client base ready to go solo, whether you occasionally do editorial work to keep yourself occupied or it's your sole means of support, HMRC will expect you to be businesslike about your finances and your obligations. It matters not a jot that you're a words person, and perhaps not a numbers one.

A word of warning: work done for payment in kind is still taxable, so if you swap proofreading services (perhaps you and a friend proofread each other's websites without a financial payment in either direction), or you copyedit your neighbour's magnum opus for a year's supply of honey and home-made wimberry pies, HMRC wants to know.[75] The payment in kind must be converted to a cash value of its worth and that figure will appear in your accounts.

Registering as self-employed

If you run your own business as an individual, you are a sole trader and self-employed. You do not need to register as a sole trader until you are earning above a specified sum,[76] although you may choose to register sooner, voluntarily, in order to keep your National Insurance record going or perhaps to claim tax-free childcare.

When you register as a sole trader, you must also set up an online account (Government Gateway) to access your business tax account to submit your self-assessment returns, check balances of tax/NICs still due and make payments.[77] You will also need your Government Gateway details to join the MTD pilot or the live system. Once you have your Government Gateway account up and running, download the HMRC app – in some ways the app is easier to use than the web-based account, having more details literally at your fingertips, especially for quickly looking things up and seeing your estimated tax bill.

The GOV.UK website explains how to decide whether you're self-employed or not for the purposes of any particular job or contract,[78,79] as freelance work can sometimes be treated as employment.

Note that it's possible to be treated by HMRC as an employee for one job (perhaps because of certain conditions from the client), but as self-employed for another. So even as a freelancer, you can be both employed and self-employed in the same tax year for doing the same kind of work. You can be hired to do a piece of work on terms that make you an employee in the eyes of HMRC, but that doesn't mean that you're not self-employed for other jobs you undertake. Or you can be employed by day and a self-employed proofreader at the weekends. HMRC is fine with that.

The test for whether you are self-employed is pretty straightforward. GOV.UK says you are probably self-employed if you do all of the following:[80]

- run your business for yourself and take responsibility for its success or failure
- have several customers at the same time
- can decide how, where and when you do your work
- can hire other people at your own expense to help you or to do the work for you
- provide the main items of equipment to do your work
- are responsible for finishing any unsatisfactory work in your own time
- charge an agreed fixed price for your work
- sell goods or services to make a profit (including through websites or apps).

The penultimate item in this list is the most contentious one. Many editorial freelancers prefer to charge an hourly rate, given scope creep and jobs taking longer (or shorter) than expected, perhaps as the result of a poor brief from the client. However, HMRC sees hourly rates as the start of the slippery slope to employment and it may be harder to justify your treatment as self-employed.

Using the tools and advice in CIEP guides, as discussed in chapter 4 **in relation to recording your own experience**, is essential to providing accurate quotations for a job that are fair to both you and your client, and will enable you to move to agreeing a fixed price with confidence.

If the terms of a contract make it impossible to justify self-employed status *for that piece of work* to HMRC, it may be that you should be treated as an employee, with tax, NICs and perhaps pension contributions taken at source under PAYE. Your employer will also have NICs and pension contributions to make on your employment, and you will get a payslip for each pay period you were employed for, with a P60 at the end of the tax year. You will need those for your tax return, where you will have to fill out both the self-employment and employee pages.

Assuming that you are self-employed for at least some of the work you're doing, you should register as self-employed *as soon as you make yourself available for work*, and in any event by 5 October of your business's second tax year (which means that if you go solo any time between April and March, you will need to register no later than the 5 October afterwards). The HMRC website guides you through the registration options and process[81,82] and there is a great deal of information produced for the newly self-employed. HMRC puts a lot of effort into helping the self-employed get things right first time, and to pay the right amount in tax and NICs and on time. Less work for them, no penalties or interest for you.

IR35 is the regulation about employment status and whether or not it is acceptable to pay people off the payroll; its use is being extended, from April 2021. Keep an eye on the **Going Solo Toolkit** for news on this.

Access to information about tax, National Insurance and self-employment

Once you are registered, you can access even more information about the process. Subscribe to the HMRC help and support emails service[83] to receive mailings that will keep you up to date with changes and offer additional help and information for sole traders and small business owners. HMRC has a YouTube channel and runs live webinars on various topics throughout the year, free of charge. Some of the webinars are recorded and you can watch them on catch-up, but attending the live version enables you to ask questions of HMRC staff direct, using the chat box. They can't answer about your own personal tax record, but they can certainly answer questions of principle relating to your circumstances.

Income tax

You will pay income tax on your *profits* each year, not your gross income, on the excess above your tax allowance. Your tax allowance will depend on your personal circumstances, and tax rules vary between the UK nations. See the **Going Solo Toolkit** for more details.

6 | Money

Business expenses

Things you buy to run your business can be offset against your income, reducing your tax bill. These are called 'allowable business expenses'. The item must be entirely used in the business, otherwise you will have to deduct the portion that is for personal use.

If you work from home, as a great many sole traders in the editorial world do, you can offset against your tax liability various allowances for the use of your home for business purposes, including a proportion of heating, lighting, broadband and phone bills.[84] HMRC introduced the simplified expenses scheme to save an awful lot of calculation and head-scratching for the household expenses (essentially utility bills), and sets out a figure you can claim each month on a sliding scale according to the number of hours worked (another reason to record these).[85] You will need to decide whether you use this simplified scheme (only available if you work at least 25 hours per month in your business) or work out your actual expenses (based on actual household bills and the space you use as an office); one method may be more beneficial than the other, but you won't know which until you have worked out the figures using both methods. There is a tool on the GOV.UK website to help you with the calculation.[86] Which you choose may depend on whether every last penny, or every last minute, is more important to you. For mortgage interest or rent, council tax, and phone and broadband costs, calculate the proportion attributable to your business.

You can also claim:

- professional memberships, such as your CIEP subscription
- training costs of CPD (but *not* training for a new specialism or to be in a position to start trading as an editor or proofreader, remember) with its associated travel (and, if it involves an overnight stay, subsistence) expenses
- stationery and computer consumables
- reference and instructional books, subscriptions to dictionaries and other resources, and so on
- capital expenditure[87] – office furniture, computer hardware.

You'll need to take care to separate the appropriate costs of some things you may have for both business and personal use – computer consumables, the computer itself, your phone. HMRC expects this proportion to be fair and reasonable, rather than costed exactly.

For the detail of what you can and can't claim as allowable business expenses, the GOV.UK website is the place to go, where you will find the HMRC's internal manual *Business Income Manual*.[88]

You can claim for things bought prior to beginning trading (up to seven years prior) that you need to start up your business – stationery, office furniture, equipment, consumables, advertising.

If you feel that the simplified expenses scheme doesn't work in your favour, you can still use the traditional expenses method. HMRC's videos and webinars, and the GOV.UK website, explain it all.[89,90]

Trading allowance

When you are starting out you may find it easier to claim the trading allowance than actual business expenses. HMRC allows you to spend up to this allowance on business expenses in a tax year, tax free. If your actual allowable business expenses come to less, you are entitled to claim the full trading allowance instead, but you can't claim more than your business income[91] (see the **Going Solo Toolkit** for more).

Deciding on your accounting year

HMRC says that the simplest business accounting year for calculating tax and NI liabilities is one that coincides with the tax year. You can reduce the length of your first accounting year to end on 5 April, and if you keep your accounts on a calendar monthly basis, you can treat 31 March as being the end of the tax year, instead of 5 April. You can run your accounting year for a full 12 months from your start date if you prefer, but you have to split your data into two tax years each time.

However, to bring taxation on profits to relate directly to the tax year in which they were earned, in 2023/24 HMRC brought in transitional rules changing the way the profit is apportioned. HMRC Help Sheet HS222, paragraph 16, explains the method (see the Resources section). New rules apply from 2024/25.

You will be asked to state on your self-assessment tax return the date to which your business accounts are made up (by which HMRC means the date of the end of your business accounting year).

National Insurance

Self-employed people pay anything from no NICs up to three classes of NICs simultaneously, depending on their profit levels and personal circumstances. Current rates and other details are available in the **Going Solo Toolkit**.

VAT

If you are a CIEP member, take a look at the **Going Solo Toolkit** for the latest detail on VAT, especially if you sell ebooks and the like through your website to customers in the EU.

Your first year in business – a warning about a bigger tax bill!

Although your tax is calculated on the figures for the tax year just ended, if the tax due is over £1,000 HMRC will also collect half of the anticipated tax (which it calls 'payments on account') for the *next* year with the initial year's payment. This is explained in more detail in the **Going Solo Toolkit**.

HMRC has a tool[92] to help you work out your likely tax and NIC bill, so you can budget for it as early as possible. Note that the tool works only if you have very simple tax affairs, and no other income.

The advantages of completing your tax return as early as possible

Personally, I complete my tax return as soon as possible, then pay my bill in monthly instalments, mimicking PAYE. While interest rates remain so low, I may as well keep my tax bill under control. Other people prefer to build up the money in a savings account and pay at the very last moment, which is fine if you have all the money ready. If you struggle to budget, consider making payments on account, during the year. You can even do this in advance of completing your first self-employed tax return. It's my personal opinion that MTD may result in a requirement for earlier payment of tax and National Insurance bills – if I'm right, keeping up to date with your tax liability as much as possible will be no bad thing and make transition easier. In terms of business robustness, having a large bill hanging over your head and relying on future income to pay it is perhaps not the most sensible approach, as many found when the pandemic struck.

Invoicing and chasing late payment

Invoices must include certain information by law[93] and it is a good idea to include on your invoice the date by which payment is due and that you reserve the right to charge interest for late payment (by another business; this law doesn't apply to private customers)[94] plus debt recovery costs.[95] Then your client is in no doubt that you expect to be paid promptly and you have made your position clear from the outset. A private client could be pursued through the small-claims court system in your jurisdiction. The law also sets out the default date an invoice is considered overdue, if no other payment terms have been agreed.[96]

I see too many posts on the forums and other social media saying how cringeworthy invoicing and pursuing payment is – asking people for money makes some editorial freelancers' toes curl. Or drawing up invoices is boring, they say. Well, you just have to get past that. If you don't value your time and skill, who should?

You're not asking for your pocket money for doing your chores. You're not asking for a favour. You are a business person who has delivered according to contract and the other half of that contract is payment for services rendered. I send my invoice with the files for most jobs – I think of it as the victory roll on completion of the job! I copyedit two scholarly journals and for those I invoice on the first working day of the month – and that is set up as a recurring appointment in my diary. You may have a different routine, but have one.

If you are charging a client a deposit in advance, or stage payments during a long job, treat those invoices the same way. Don't start the work hoping for the best if the deposit hasn't cleared your bank account. See chapter 3 for more information on language to use in your **T&Cs**.

If you have to chase payment, record each contact regarding non-payment. Remain polite, but don't let the matter ride. You're running a business. Get your invoices out promptly and make it clear when payment is due. Record this. On the day after an invoice falls due, chase non-payment.

Be businesslike and your client will (usually) respond in the same way. Don't be shy about threatening the recalcitrant with recourse to the courts for debt recovery. You may risk torpedoing your future relationship with that client, but if you are struggling to get your invoices paid, you may not mind that.[97] In England and Wales, county court judgments stay on record for six years and most clients will want to avoid the embarrassment. If you do find yourself having to rattle your sabre to be paid, check out a website like Late Payment Law for additional guidance.[98]

Should you be a company?

Some freelancers – even sole traders – have set themselves up as companies. There is more involved in that decision than this guide can cover, and there are tax and legal implications, all the more so with the extension of IR35 to the private sector.

Do you see yourself as working alone and accepting only work that you know you will carry out yourself? Do you see yourself instead as being the focal point of getting work in, but employing others to provide at least some of the services? Is your market a high-risk one or one that expects to deal with organisations rather than individuals? It's probable that registering your business as a company from the outset is unnecessarily expensive and complex, but, depending on your ambitions, it may be something you should read up on and prepare for.

Do you need an accountant?

I'm afraid that there's no simple answer! A great many people do perfectly well without one. You may, though, find it worthwhile to employ an accountant for the first year or two to help you form good habits and to get advice on things such as business expenses. You may find it rather more worthwhile to use an accountant every year if your tax affairs are in any way complex. Accountancy fees are an allowable business expense.

Bank accounts

It's not necessary to have a separate business bank account, in the UK. You may find it easier to have one, though, especially if you have lots of smaller jobs resulting in lots of payments. Otherwise be sure to mark the invoice or receipt number on your personal bank statements for all income and outgoings related to your business, and keep these with your tax records.

Having online banking facilities will mean you can easily check whether invoices are paid on time, and move money to savings accounts.

If you are going to be working with overseas clients, you might need an account that allows you to accept payment in other currencies as cheaply as possible, although bank fees are allowable business expenses. This facility and cost are worth investigating when choosing a bank account.

You can offer other payment methods to your clients, in addition to bank transfers. PayPal is a popular choice as it allows clients to use a debit or credit card, although there are transaction fees to pay.[99] An alternative is TransferWise. CIEP members can search the forums for up-to-date discussion on other methods. And remember – cheques are not quite dead yet, but do bear in mind that they are not a particularly secure method of payment.

7| You

Taking care of yourself

Working as a self-employed editorial professional can be hard on the body and on the mind. You may find yourself working for longer stretches of time without a break, or seeing other people far less often than you have been used to. It makes good sense to look after yourself as well as you can: you *are* your business.

The basic set-up

Ergonomics and repetitive strain injury (RSI)

You may well be spending longer at your desk for uninterrupted periods than you ever have before, and putting yourself at risk of RSI. It's essential that you equip yourself with the best working environment that you can. Take a look at recommendations for healthy arrangements of your office space.[100] Make sure you are sitting well, without straining eyes, neck, shoulders, arms or back. The UK's Chartered Society of Physiotherapy has information about avoiding workplace injury and exercises to do at your desk,[101] and the NHS has good advice on sitting safely.[102] The Health and Safety Executive also offers advice.[103]

Your choice of mouse is also of great importance if you want to prevent carpal tunnel syndrome. Some people find it helps to switch the hand they use for the mouse (experiment with changing the button assignments if you do that). Investigate different shapes of mouse, including the baseball-shaped ones, vertical mice, stationary trackballs and tablets with pens.

It's now known that sitting for extended periods is injurious to your health, so it's important to take regular breaks from your work and get yourself moving. Standing desks are becoming more popular, but if that's not for you, explore the world of seated exercise, with under-desk ellipticals and similar gizmos to keep your circulation going.

Some people work entirely on a laptop, but you can expand it and make yourself more comfortable – and work more safely – if you add on a mouse, a full-size keyboard and a larger monitor. You can get laptop stands that mean that you're not working looking down into the monitor, and the keyboard is on a slant to avoid wrist strain.

See chapter 7 for places to find **ergonomic furniture and equipment**.

People with disabilities

The Access to Work scheme[104] can help pay to set up a home office if you have a condition that requires you to have special equipment. Paula Gilfillan wrote on this in *Editing Matters*.[105]

Time management

It's essential that you keep track of how you spend your time, to improve efficiency, reduce stress and learn how long various tasks take you.

There are many facets to managing your time. You will need to record the time you spend working, for all the reasons previously discussed. You can track your time on a piece of paper, just writing down your starting and stopping times, and what you were working on, then adding up the time spent. You may build a spreadsheet with the time marked into blocks of 5, 10 or 15 minutes. And there are apps that will help you track your time for billing purposes. See chapter 7 for a list of **time-tracking apps**.

Do use some sort of diary, not just to mark deadlines and schedule time for working, but to remind you to do all sorts of tasks – periodic computer housekeeping and security, raising monthly invoices if you have those for any clients, updating your accounts, tax-related deadlines (with a reminder timed so you don't miss them). If you find yourself forgetting to update your social media, or read the CIEP forums, put that in your diary, too. Using a diary means referring to it daily, as well as just filling it in.

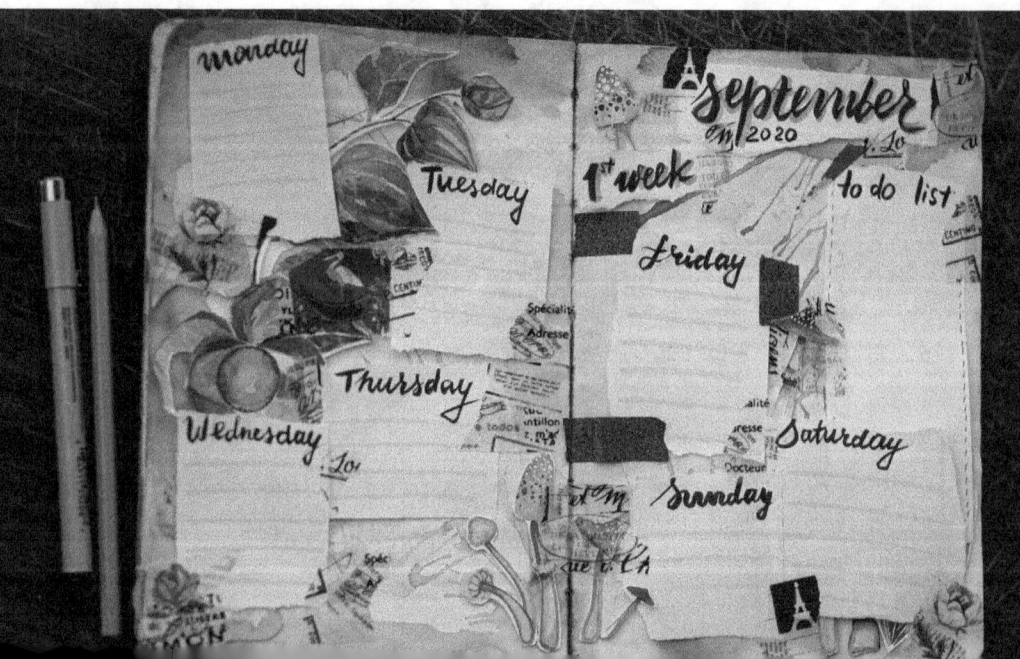

Develop an end-of-day ritual to take the place of the commute as the break between work-you and you-you. Update your timesheets and other records; check for any invoices about to go overdue and note them on your to-do list as a high priority; look over your schedule for tomorrow and add any last-minute thoughts to it; back up today's work, your record sheets and any invoices issued.

At the end of the last day of your working week, look over your diary for the following week, or draw one up, and ensure that it has everything on it that it should have – *all* your time commitments and your deadlines. Then log off and go and do something else, or nothing at all!

When it comes to looking at how you actually spend your time at your desk, you may find you need to force yourself to take breaks, or you may need to force yourself to work! Too many or too few breaks can create stress and other health problems. There are **many apps to help keep you focused**, and several are listed in chapter 7 for you to explore and see what works for you. Some will tell you when to take a break, some of them even suggest exercises you can do and still others will keep you away from social media, if you find that you're spending more time on Facebook than on the work you should be doing.

> *Don't be distracted by things around the house (entertainment, a succession of chores, other occupants) or the greater freedom to indulge in the time sink of social media. Ensure you are disciplined and stay focused on your work. It is essential to ring fence the time you spend on your breaks.*
>
> Steve Garnsey

To help keep concentration high, many people like to use the Pomodoro Technique,[106] with, say, a 5-minute break after 25 minutes of work, with a longer break after a couple of hours. Even if you think you'd prefer to knuckle down and work in longer stretches to avoid having your concentration broken, it's worth experimenting with this. You may surprise yourself. Just like when taking a decent lunch break, the gains in being fresher outweigh the absolute loss of time.

Do guard against working all the time. It's not healthy, and if you routinely work crazy hours, what will you do when there's some kind of crisis with a job or a client, or in your own life? Beware of presenteeism, which is as prevalent in the self-employed as among employees with an unenlightened boss – always being 'on' and hanging around your computer just in case a job offer comes in, living some kind of half-life. Don't be the unenlightened boss of yourself!

Equally difficult is Parkinson's Law – that work expands to fill the time available. If you have no work to do, do something else. It may be deliberately work-related – doing some training, catching up with editorial blogs, forums and other social media, progressing your marketing, updating your accounts – or it may not.

When you have finished the work on your desk, or your training time, or your blog-reading, stop work. Get up and move around, change your focus physically and mentally. Go for a walk (and contribute to #stetwalk on Twitter), pursue your hobby (and try to ensure some of your hobbies don't have you connected to your computer for even longer), clean the fridge, visit a friend (or be visited without watching the clock), watch a movie in the morning or lose yourself in a good book ... When you're at work, be at work. When you're not, make that distinction. There is more to life, and to being your own boss, than work.

Support from others

If you find yourself working alone, as most editorial freelancers do, take care to interact with people and set up support structures for your own wellbeing. Post-Covid, many more people will be aware of what working at home means, and it will be interesting to see how this pans out. I hope that more support will become available.

Professional networking organisations seem to be on the increase. Some are free, some require a fee. There is a **networking starter list** in chapter 7.

> **Be circumspect about much that is said on Facebook and other social media. Learn early who/what is a reliable and respected source of information.**
>
> Janet MacMillan

Some freelancers like to work in shared workspaces, from popping into their local café once in a while to renting co-working space in offices designed to bring freelancers together, to reduce feelings of isolation.[107,108]

Online communities give you a great place to chat with other editorial professionals, as discussed in chapter 2. Facebook groups and the CIEP forums are perfect for this; they are also good sources of support and advice if you're unsure how to handle a situation with a client or potential client (take care to preserve confidentiality – you never know who is reading). Less on demand, but with the benefit of involving facetime with real people, are CIEP local groups, local writers' groups and networking events.

Make time for friends and family, and think about how you schedule your work, so that you don't cut yourself off. Feeling part of a community and in touch with the world is one of the pillars of wellbeing.[109]

Dealing with criticism and imposter syndrome

With the best will in the world, you can't please all of the people all of the time. Clients will kick back either with or without good reason. When this happens, it's an astonishingly emotional thing.

> *Keep a 'win jar' (or digital equivalent) of positive feedback that you receive. There will be times when you doubt yourself, and it can be good to dip into to remind yourself that you do in fact know what you are doing.*

Sue Browning

Avoid having unhappy clients as much as you can by concentrating on excellent customer service (along with everything else).[110,111,112] If you do end up coping with a critical customer, don't react in haste; seek support on the CIEP forums or other *discreet* social media (so the EAE Backroom, rather than the main Editors' Association of Earth group, on Facebook) and don't be bounced into anything. Consider calmly whether any part of the criticism is justified. If it is, make the appropriate amends. If the criticism is not justified (of the type, 'My ex-boyfriend's mother's cousin read half a short story once and he's now read mine and thinks your edits are rubbish', or 'How dare you change "should of" to "should have"? You know nothing!' or, perhaps worst of all, 'Grammarly [or Editor, in Word] found loads of things you missed!'), take the time to read the advice you are given before responding, and give it careful consideration – don't send a knee-jerk response you may well regret when your blood has cooled (top tip: while drafting an email in reply, leave the 'To' box blank until you really are ready to hit 'Send'). Remember that CIEP members are bound by their Code of Practice, and the Complaints Procedure[113] route may satisfy both client and editor/proofreader if there is a serious problem.

Imposter syndrome is rife among freelancers.[114] We all doubt ourselves from time to time, but it's how you pick yourself up again that matters. Even the most experienced and well-trained editorial professionals can worry that they're about to be found out. The main thing is to recognise it for what it is. If you can point to a legitimate failing in your performance, fine. (Re)train in that topic, update your processes and determine to do better. If invalid criticism has brought on these feelings, talk them over with friends and peers rather than allow them to take up long-term residence in your head. Take comfort from the fact you are certainly not alone in feeling this way from time to time.

IT security

Be very aware of how many horrible people out there are phishing for your personal details, trying to trick you into installing malware on your computer and trying to steal your money. Approach each email with caution. Don't click on links within emails. If you're tempted, use your search engine to find the right link and connect from there. Hover your mouse over each link and see if the address is correct. Often it will be obvious the link is not what it purports to be. Sometimes the address will look valid – but it may be out by a hyphen or a single character. If there's an attachment from an author don't open it until you've exchanged a few emails and are confident the sender is acting in good faith. And then scan the document for malware before you open it. Better safe than sorry.

Other scams include 'overpaying' by cheque, asking you to refund the difference, then stopping the cheque so you have not only done work for free, you've handed over some of your own money to the scammer.[115]

Scammers will also pretend to be HMRC[116] either wanting information from you or offering you a lovely tax refund if only you will click on the link and give lots of personal information.

Cybersecurity crops up from time to time on the CIEP forums[117] and people are happy to contribute their latest findings, so keep an eye out for such posts.

Finally, think about setting Google alerts[118] for your business name and your own name, so you can keep an eye out for any untoward mentions. Use Copyscape[119] periodically to check that no one has plagiarised the text from your website, and if you have a headshot on your website and social media, also check periodically via a reverse image search[120] that no one has purloined that.

Business resilience

Building business resilience (including disaster planning) is like insurance – you hope you'll never need it, but you know you should have it, just in case. And again like insurance, disaster planning needs to be in place before you need it, if it is to reduce your stress levels at the most stressful time and give you any chance of dealing with the issues effectively.

First rule of building resilience: anticipate problems and lay plans.

First rule of being on the edge of disaster: don't panic.[121] It may not be quite as bad as you think. Breathe and think before you react.

Probably the most common disaster is your own ill-health at a crucial point in a job, or a persistent health problem that affects your ability to deliver to your clients. Your computer may also fail abruptly, or may be infected by malware. Other disasters include fire or flood affecting your home, as your office will also go up in smoke or under the waters. You may be bereaved, or have a loved one in hospital, or a childcare, eldercare or pet-care emergency that takes you away from your desk for too long and wrecks your ability to concentrate.

I'm prone to migraines, so I schedule two migraine days into every (book-length) job. If you have a chronic issue, be realistic about how many hours you can work productively per day, and how many days per week (see chapter 3 for more on **scheduling** a 'standard' working day and adjust yours down according to your needs and abilities).

Protect your computer with an antivirus program (yes, even if you have a Mac) and use it. Add one, or preferably two, anti-malware programs, as no single program will find everything. Search online for "best [Mac or PC] malware protection" for up-to-date recommendations. But be aware that you may get performance issues if you load too many, or choose a pair that don't play nicely together. Keep the software up to date – accept automatic (and frequent) updates – and keep it running in the background. Make sure it's set to start up when you switch on your computer. If you're fact-checking, you will end up on all kinds of websites. Some of them are bound to turn out to be regrettable or compromised. Set your firewall as tightly as you can until just before it actually stops you from doing what you need.

Backing up your work is critical. Consider cloud storage *with live back-up*.[122] Popular ISPs offer a certain amount of storage free in their packages, with more available for a fee. Dropbox is also very popular. Microsoft 365 includes OneDrive. Backing up files elsewhere than on your computer is essential if you are to recover quickly from a computer failure or infection. Remember to include your emails, which are usually stored in a different location from your document files, and any files such as photos and videos that are saved in other folders or locations.

To back up on your computer, set up Windows File History[123] or Apple Time Machine.[124] Also back up onto an external hard drive or USB drive as you prefer, or as space demands. Back up a recovery system image of your computer twice and keep one copy offsite where you can access it easily should you need it; with a friend, perhaps. Keep the onsite copy in your firebox, if you have one (see '**Statutory records**' in chapter 4).

Refresh a specific back-up of your browser settings and favourites, contacts, to-do list, bookmarks, passwords, ribbon customisation and so on routinely, onto external media. If your computer dies and you need to replace it, being able to import all these features will get you up and running efficiently much more quickly than having to work it all out again. Instructions will be particular to your browser, so a spot of online searching is in order on how to do this. What seems a fiddle at first will soon become easy, through familiarity.

Some people email files to themselves, so there's a copy on their ISP's server. Check that neither your settings nor those of your ISP delete emails from the ISP's server as soon as they're delivered to your computer if you choose this route. It also doubles as a method of version control for documents.

Find a computer repair service *before* you need it – ask for recommendations, or at least collect more than one number – and store the details where you won't lose them.

> *Ask around for recommendations for a reliable IT wizard for those times when your IT problem-solving skills, and those of your nearest and dearest, aren't enough.*
>
> Annie Jackson

If you can afford it, the luxury of a spare keyboard, mouse, monitor, computer and printer is great (as long as you still have access to your home, of course). Keep the spare computer updated if you don't want to be tearing your hair out when you finally switch it on and need to use it in an emergency, only to have 18 months' worth of software updates take over. And never run out of spare batteries for mouse and keyboard, if you use wireless kit.

Planning for the worst

Should the very worst happen, will your family or friends know what to do about your business? The CIEP has some resources to help you think through the preparations you need to make while you are fit and well, and the information you need to make available to your executor. See **'Business resilience'** in chapter 7.

Professional indemnity insurance

You should assess your risks and decide whether such insurance is right for you. At the time of writing, PolicyBee[125] is the CIEP's partner insurer,[126] and is offering discounted cyber liability insurance as well as professional indemnity insurance. There are many other providers in the market, however, which you can find online and compare prices and coverage. Some clients will require you to have professional indemnity insurance. If you do decide to buy insurance, check that your policy covers all the countries or regions where you are likely to have clients. Geographical exclusions can sneak in and make your policy worthless.

Upgrading CIEP membership and other goals

If you previously worked in an area where promotion was a possibility, and something to work towards, that disappears when you start to work for yourself.

One way to replicate – to some degree – the feeling of accomplishment that comes with a promotion is to work your way up the CIEP grades: Entry-Level, Intermediate, Professional and Advanced Professional. All members have the right to have on their website a CIEP badge showing their grade. The full list of membership benefits is on the CIEP website.[127] Remember that there is a time limit before you must upgrade from the Entry-Level/Intermediate Member grades to the professional grades, so upgrading should be in your thoughts from the outset. Members should download the Member Handbook, which gives more information on the upgrading system, including the time limits.[128]

Or set yourself other goals, perhaps joining networking groups. Take a look at the section '**Continuing professional development**' in chapter 2 for ideas to keep you focused and moving forward. Working for yourself gives you the freedom to build your business and your career in the way that suits you best, but it's also easy just to keep going at the same level, which can make you feel as if you're in a rut. Investing in yourself is directly investing in your business. Sara Donaldson has given advice on her blog on how to choose a CPD course.[129]

I hope that following the advice in this guide will make it easier for you to navigate the many things you have to think about when going solo, and help get you up and running smoothly as you embark on this new phase of your career. I wish you good luck!

8 | Resources

All URLs are correct as at the time of publication. CIEP members can find an updated list in the **Going Solo Toolkit** on our website.

Being a freelancer
theserialistblog.wordpress.com

Business planning
Writing a business plan: **gov.uk/write-business-plan** – includes downloadable templates as well as advice.

COBRA Business Opportunity Profiles – Editorial Service:
forums.ciep.uk/read.php?12,208533

Support for small businesses: **gov.uk/browse/business**

Local business start-up support discussion (CIEP members only):
forums.ciep.uk/read.php?12,189995,189995#msg-189995

IPSE (Association of Independent Professionals and the Self-Employed) is a membership organisation giving support in various areas to freelancers:
ipse.co.uk

AIPP (Association of Independent Publishing Professionals) was founded in 2016 to support freelancers working with indie authors and small publishing houses:
aipponline.org

Louise Harnby: *Business Planning for Editorial Freelancers*
louiseharnbyproofreader.com/business-planning-for-editorial-freelancers-a-guide-for-new-starters.html

Find your local chamber of commerce: **britishchambers.org.uk**

This 2016 independent report on self-employment commissioned by the government may also be of interest (I've not been able to find anything more recent that's comparable): **gov.uk/government/uploads/system/uploads/attachment_data/file/529702/ind-16-2-self-employment-review.pdf**

Business networking
Sara Donaldson has tried out three networking organisations: **northerneditorial.co.uk/2020/05/16/why-you-need-a-freelance-support-network**

BookMachine offers two levels of membership (with or without events): **bookmachine.org**

Branding
John Espirian: *Content DNA* **espirian.co.uk/book**

Louise Harnby: *How to Brand Your Editing Business* **louiseharnbyproofreader.com/how-to-brand-your-editing-business.html**

Louise Harnby: Branding for Business Growth online training course **louiseharnbyproofreader.com/blog/branding-for-business-growth-new-online-course-for-editors-and-proofreaders**

Lindsay Marsh, *The Personal Branding Process for Creative Freelancers* **skillshare.com/classes/The-Personal-Branding-Process-for-Creative-Freelancers/1837378792**

Marketing
CIEP guide: Sara Hulse, *Marketing Yourself: Strategies to promote your editorial business* **ciep.uk/resources/guides/#MY**

CIEP suggested minimum rates: **ciep.uk/resources/suggested-minimum-rates**

Louise Harnby, *Marketing Your Editing & Proofreading Business* **louiseharnbyproofreader.com/marketing-your-editing--proofreading-business.html**

The law on marketing and advertising: **gov.uk/marketing-advertising-law**

Cold-calling advice: **theguardian.com/small-business-network/2016/jan/07/introverts-succeed-sales-prepation-cold-calling**

CIEP
CIEP website: **ciep.uk**

CIEP practice notes: **ciep.uk/resources/factsheets**

Editorial Excellence, a free email newsletter on working with editors and proofreaders for anyone to subscribe to: **ciep.uk/resources/newsletters**

8 | Resources

For CIEP members:

To access items in the members' area, you will need to log in first.

The Edit: **ciep.uk/resources/newsletters/the-edit**

Editing Matters archive: **ciep.uk/members/communicating/editing-matters/editing-matters-archive**

Editing Matters index: **ciep.uk/resources/newsletters/editing-matters/index**

The forums: **forums.ciep.uk/index.php**. Once you've registered, click on your name at the top of the page and follow the links to join additional forums.

Ergonomic furniture, mice and keyboards

officefurnitureonline.co.uk/office-chairs/posture-ergonomic-office-chairs/

healthyworkstations.com

posturite.co.uk/ergonomic-mice-keyboards/ergonomic-keyboards.html

posturite.co.uk/ergonomic-accessories/ergonomic-mice.html

ergonomics.co.uk (See also benefits in the CIEP members' area for discounts, guidance and exercises)

Preventing workplace injury

For a fuller explanation of RSI:
nhs.uk/conditions/Repetitive-strain-injury/Pages/Introduction.aspx

On back pain at work: **nhs.uk/conditions/back-pain**

How to sit correctly: **nhs.uk/live-well/healthy-body/how-to-sit-correctly**

Using a laptop safely:
nhs.uk/live-well/healthy-body/posture-tips-for-laptop-users

Common posture mistakes and fixes:
nhs.uk/live-well/exercise/common-posture-mistakes-and-fixes

Tax and National Insurance, VAT, MTD, IR35

HMRC's key help, including signing up for routine help and support emails
gov.uk/government/collections/hmrc-webinars-email-alerts-and-videos

HMRC YouTube channel: **youtube.com/user/HMRCgovuk**

Contact HMRC: **gov.uk/contact-hmrc**

Self-employed helpline number: 0300 200 3500

National Insurance for the self-employed: gov.uk/government/organisations/hm-revenue-customs/contact/national-insurance-enquiries-for-the-self-employed

VAT helpline: 0300 200 3700 gov.uk/government/organisations/hm-revenue-customs/contact/vat-enquiries

Self-employment and HMRC – getting started

Running a business from home: **gov.uk/run-business-from-home**

How to register with HMRC: **gov.uk/new-business-register-for-tax**

Starting your own business: **hmrc.gov.uk/courses/SYOB3/syob_3/html/syob_3_menu.html**

Self-employed and claiming Universal Credit: **gov.uk/self-employment-and-universal-credit**

Business expenses

Allowable professional subscriptions (aka 'List 3'): **gov.uk/government/publications/professional-bodies-approved-for-tax-relief-list-3** (the CIEP is included)

Capital or revenue? **gov.uk/hmrc-internal-manuals/business-income-manual/bim35000**

What is and isn't allowable? **gov.uk/hmrc-internal-manuals/business-income-manual/bim42526**

More info on 'cost of sales' (HS222): **gov.uk/government/publications/how-to-calculate-your-taxable-profits-hs222-self-assessment-helpsheet**

Simplified expenses: **gov.uk/simpler-income-tax-simplified-expenses**

What does 'wholly and exclusively' mean? **gov.uk/hmrc-internal-manuals/business-income-manual/bim42105**

Travel and subsistence information: **gov.uk/hmrc-internal-manuals/business-income-manual/bim47705**

Calculating your tax and NICs liability

How to calculate your taxable profit: **gov.uk/government/publications/how-to-calculate-your-taxable-profits-hs222-self-assessment-helpsheet**

How to get your SA302 (evidence of earnings for the last four years, needed for mortgage applications and similar) tax calculation: **gov.uk/sa302-tax-calculation**

Tax allowances and reliefs: **gov.uk/expenses-if-youre-self-employed**

Current tax and NI rates: **gov.uk/government/collections/rates-and-allowances-hm-revenue-and-customs**

Ready reckoner: **gov.uk/self-assessment-ready-reckoner**

Money Advice Service summary of tax and NICs for the self-employed: **moneyadviceservice.org.uk/en/articles/tax-and-national-insurance-when-youre-self-employed**

Keeping your pay and tax records for self-assessment
gov.uk/keeping-your-pay-tax-records/overview

Information on record-keeping: **gov.uk/self-employed-records**

Keeping VAT records: **gov.uk/vat-record-keeping**

Mobile record-keeping apps
gov.uk/government/publications/record-keeping-and-simpler-income-tax-applicationssoftware

Info on mobile apps: gov.uk/government/collections/record-keeping-and-simpler-income-tax-applicationssoftware

Use of home as office
Tax relief for use of home for business: gov.uk/hmrc-internal-manuals/business-income-manual/bim47805

Examples: gov.uk/hmrc-internal-manuals/business-income-manual/bim47825

Valuation Office Agency advice on working from home and council tax: gov.uk/introduction-to-business-rates/working-at-home

Invoicing and pursuing payment

Content of invoices
gov.uk/invoicing-and-taking-payment-from-customers/invoices-what-they-must-include

Charging interest on late payment on commercial invoices

gov.uk/late-commercial-payments-interest-debt-recovery/charging-interest-commercial-debt

Planning and time management

Tracking your time

cushionapp.com (see also blog.ciep.uk/systematising)

quickbooks.intuit.com/uk

timesheet.io/en

toggl.com/track

officetime.net

timecamp.com

blueskyapp.com (an accounting app with a built-in time tracker)

dualitysoft.com/dsclock

freshbooks.com (an accounting package with a built-in time tracker)

getharvest.com

getklok.com

timestamp.io

trello.com/en

zoho.com/uk/invoice (an accounting solution with time tracker)

To help you keep focused

goodhousekeeping.com/life/g32714945/best-productivity-apps

freedom.to

proginosko.com/leechblock

focusme.co/features

chrome.google.com/webstore/detail/stayfocusd/laankejkbhbdhmipfmgcngdelahlfoji

selfcontrolapp.com (for Macs)

To remind you to take breaks

tomato-timer.com

A review of several apps:
umsystem.edu/totalrewards/wellness/activity_and_break_apps

Non-distracting background sounds

Many editors work in silence, and others to non-vocal music. A few manage to listen to the radio or 'ordinary' music, but if that's not for you, try: **noisli.com**

On **youtube.com**, search for "nature sounds", "concentration music" or "study music"

If you find cat purrs restful, then you can mix your own here: **mynoise.net/NoiseMachines/catPurrNoiseGenerator.php**

Skills and knowledge

The complete National Occupational Standards (2012) for the publishing arena are more easily found here than on the NOS website itself:
publishingtrainingcentre.co.uk/images/BookJournalPublishingNationalStandards.pdf

Courses from the CIEP: **ciep.uk/training/choose-a-course**

Courses from the Publishing Training Centre:
publishingtrainingcentre.co.uk/courses

Proofreading PDFs:
bookmachine.org/2015/12/07/pdf-proofreading-essential-first-step-checks

blog.catchthesun.net/2019/02/pdf-markup-basics-for-proofreaders-copyeditors

ultimateproof.co.uk/proofreading-and-marking-up-a-pdf

Stamps of BSI symbols for marking up PDFs are available from:

> Claire Ruben: **faircopy.co.uk/downloads.html**
>
> Louise Harnby: **louiseharnbyproofreader.com/blog/free-downloadable-pdf-proofreading-stamps**
>
> and also read: **louiseharnbyproofreader.com/blog/how-to-use-pdf-proofreading-stamps-on-colour-and-greyscale-pages**

CIEP curriculum: **ciep.uk/training/about-ciep-training-courses/curriculum**

CIEP guides: **ciep.uk/resources/guides**

CIEP focus papers and fact sheets: **ciep.uk/resources/factsheets** (some of these are available only to members, others to anyone, so CIEP members should be logged in to access the full list)

The Editorial Freelancers Association (EFA; US) guides: **lulu.com/spotlight/editorialfreelancers**

EFA courses: **the-efa.org/product-category/active-courses**

Editors Canada range of guides: **editors.ca/editors-canada-publications**

Editors Canada courses: **editors.ca/train-editors-association-canada-editing-experts**

Institute of Professional Editors (IPEd; Australia/New Zealand) accreditation: **iped-editors.org/Accreditation.aspx**

Liminal Pages (Sophie Playle) runs fiction-editing courses: **liminalpages.com/courses/**

Louise Harnby offers paid and free courses on editing and on running your business: **louiseharnbyproofreader.com/training-courses.html**

Louise Harnby and Denise Cowle offer The Editing Podcast, mostly on editing and writing: **youtube.com/c/TheEditingPodcast**

Places to ask peers questions

For CIEP members, the CIEP forums, of course: **forums.ciep.uk/index.php**

And, if you choose wisely, **facebook.com**. Facebook groups to consider joining include The Unofficial CIEP, Editors' Association of Earth (EAE), EAE Backroom (a closed group, where your questions and comments won't be indexed so won't pop up to embarrass you in web search results), Conferences for Editors, EAE Ad Space, Academic Editors, Fiction Writers and Editors, and Certifications for Copyeditors, for starters.

The Editors Lair: **editorslair.com**

Editorial tools

Paul Beverley's macros: **archivepub.co.uk/Macros.html**

Jack Lyon's books:

> *Wildcard Cookbook for Microsoft Word*, ISBN 9781434103987 **amzn.to/32mlw8o**

> *Macro Cookbook for Microsoft Word*, ISBN 9781434103321 **amzn.to/3lj7BIX**

Geoff Hart, *Effective Onscreen Editing*, 4th edn, **ciep.uk/members/benefits/effective-onscreen-editing** (in the members' area)

WordTips for wrangling Word: **wordribbon.tips.net** for Word 2007 onwards

Hilary Cadman provides a tips and tools email newsletter for editors. Sign up here (at the foot of the Tech Tools for Editors section): **cadmantraining.com**

Cadman Training courses on EndNote: **cadmantraining.com/courses/category/EndNote%20for%20Editors**

PerfectIt: **intelligentediting.com**

Intelligent Editing, which produces PerfectIt, has a YouTube channel with tutorials: **youtube.com/user/IntelligentEditing**

Hilary Cadman also has online courses on PerfectIt: **cadmantraining.com/courses/category/PerfectIt%20for%20PC**

ACES PerfectIt webinars: **aces.mclms.net/en/package/1607/course/2655/view**

The Editorium: **editorium.com** (for the Editor's Toolkit and more)

Kutools: **extendoffice.com/product/kutools-for-word.html**

Text expanders can help if you find you're typing the same query over and over – in effect, a sophisticated version of autocompletion. Some can be found at:

> textexpander.com

> nch.com.au/fastfox

> phraseexpress.com

Computer tech

To enable your Mac to run Windows programs: **parallels.com/uk**

John Espirian's blog: **espirian.co.uk/blog** is a great source for tech help and ideas, especially for Mac users. He is on Vimeo, too: **vimeo.com/espirian**

Social media

John Espirian also is a LinkedIn guru: **espirian.co.uk/linkedin**

Manage your social media presence using organisational and scheduling tools:

> **bluleadz.com/blog/best-free-social-media-management-tools**
>
> Hootsuite: **hootsuite.com**
>
> Buffer: **buffer.com**
>
> TweetDeck: **tweetdeck.twitter.com**
> and alternatives: **agorapulse.com/blog/7-tweetdeck-alternatives**

Mark Schaeffer, *The Tao of Twitter*, 4th edn, ISBN 9780692950746 **amzn.to/2DZISsi**

Business resilience

Various blog posts and two CIEP fact sheets look at this issue (members only):
ciep.uk/resources/factsheets/#WWH
ciep.uk/resources/factsheets/#BRP

Check the list of fact sheets here for other new arrivals:
ciep.uk/resources/factsheets

blog.ciep.uk/succession-planning-for-your-business-after-you-die
americaneditor.wordpress.com/2020/02/05/on-the-basics-starting-the-new-year-by-planning-for-emergencies

forums.ciep.uk/read.php?2,230726

And this book has been recommended on the CIEP forums:

> Jane Duncan Rogers, *Before I Go: The essential guide to creating a good end of life plan*, ISBN 9781844097500 **amzn.to/2EsQpQd**

References

1. gov.uk/write-business-plan
2. blog.ciep.uk/transferable-skills
3. gov.uk/how-to-register-a-trade-mark
4. canva.com
5. Such as: psychotactics.com
6. ciep.uk/standards/code-of-practice
7. ambius.co.uk/blog/top-10-best-plants-for-your-desk-at-work/index.html
8. groundology.co.uk/earthing/grounding-mats
9. ciep.uk/members/benefits/membership-logos
10. ukstandards.org.uk/NOS-Finder#k=pub19
11. ukstandards.org.uk/NOS-Finder#k=pub20
12. ciep.uk/standards/editorial-syllabus
13. ciep.uk/resources/factsheets/#TPC
14. ciep.uk/training/mentoring
15. ciep.uk/resources/forums/about
16. ciep.uk/training/choose-a-course/practical-mark-up-of-pdfs
17. ciep.uk/resources/factsheets/#REF
18. amazon.co.uk/?ie=UTF8&link_code=hom&tag=societyforedi-21
19. en.wikipedia.org/wiki/List_of_style_guides#General
20. bbc.co.uk/academy/en/collections/news-style-guide
21. gov.uk/guidance/style-guide/a-to-z-of-gov-uk-style
22. buzzfeed.com/emmyf/buzzfeed-style-guide
23. asd-ste100.org
24. scientificstyleandformat.org/Home.html
25. ciep.uk/resources/guides/#YHS

26 ciep.uk/resources/forums/help/joining-a-forum-group
27 facebook.com/groups/EditorsofEarth
28 facebook.com/groups/usfep
29 editorslair.com
30 thebookseller.com
31 publishingperspectives.com
32 ciep.uk/networking/local
33 kokedit.com/ckb.php
34 consciousstyleguide.com
35 ciep.uk/resources/factsheets/#GFC
36 writersandartists.co.uk/listings
37 ciep.uk/resources/factsheets/#WWP
38 ciep.uk/resources/guides/#TD
39 ciep.uk/members/getting-work/directory (in the members' area)
40 ciep.uk/members/getting-work/im-available (in the members' area)
41 publishingtrainingcentre.co.uk/freelance-finder
42 ciep.uk/about/faqs/what-is-proofreading
43 best10ecommercesitebuilders.com/charts/14/best-e-commerce-site-builders
44 freelanceuk.com/technology/advice_register_domain_name.shtml
45 gov.uk/marketing-advertising-law/direct-marketing
46 gov.uk/government/publications/guide-to-the-general-data-protection-regulation
47 futurelearn.com/courses/digital-skills-digital-marketing
48 Locate your local chamber at britishchambers.org.uk
49 bookmachine.org
50 societyofauthors.org/about-us
51 allianceindependentauthors.org
52 mindtools.com/pages/article/elevator-pitch.htm
53 ciep.uk/resources/suggested-minimum-rates
54 ciep.uk/resources/guides/#PP

References

55 americaneditor.wordpress.com
56 year-planner-calendar.co.uk/year-planner-wall-diary-calendar-public-holiday-chart-academic-fiscal-free.htm
57 ciep.uk/standards/code-of-practice
58 ciep.uk/resources/top-tips
59 ciep.uk/resources/factsheets
60 ciep.uk/members/contracts/model-terms-and-conditions
61 ciep.uk/members/benefits/legal-help (in the members' area)
62 Karin Cather and Dick Margulis, *The Paper It's Written On: Defining your relationship with an editing client* ISBN 9781726073295 amzn.to/2Yi9X0R
63 theserialistblog.wordpress.com/2018/04/16/how-to-stay-safe-in-freelance-business and theserialistblog.wordpress.com/2018/04/30/how-to-stay-safe-in-freelance-business-protecting-yourself
64 gov.uk/self-employed-records/what-records-to-keep
65 A selection can be found here: amzn.to/2PZ6bF1
66 ciep.uk/members/benefits/freeagent
67 gov.uk/self-employed-records/how-long-to-keep-your-records
68 ciep.uk/resources/factsheets/#EJL
69 www.ciep.uk/members/going-solo-toolkit-uk-tax-for-freelancers
70 liminalpages.com/year-in-review-and-goals-for-2020-free-workbook-for-freelance-editors
71 whatimeantosay.com/tea.html
72 gov.uk/plan-retirement-income/overview
73 yourpension.gov.uk/self-employment
74 gov.uk/government/organisations/hm-revenue-customs/contact/self-assessment
75 gov.uk/simpler-income-tax-cash-basis/income-and-expenses-under-cash-basis
76 gov.uk/set-up-sole-trader
77 gov.uk/log-in-register-hmrc-online-services
78 gov.uk/working-for-yourself/what-counts-as-self-employed

79 gov.uk/guidance/check-employment-status-for-tax
80 gov.uk/working-for-yourself
81 gov.uk/set-up-sole-trader/register
82 gov.uk/browse/business
83 gov.uk/government/collections/hmrc-webinars-email-alerts-and-videos
84 gov.uk/expenses-if-youre-self-employed
85 gov.uk/simpler-income-tax-simplified-expenses
86 gov.uk/simplified-expenses-checker
87 gov.uk/capital-allowances
88 gov.uk/hmrc-internal-manuals/business-income-manual/bim47820
89 gov.uk/expenses-if-youre-self-employed
90 gov.uk/government/news/webinars-and-videos-about-self-assessment
91 gov.uk/guidance/tax-free-allowances-on-property-and-trading-income
92 gov.uk/self-assessment-ready-reckoner
93 gov.uk/invoicing-and-taking-payment-from-customers/invoices-what-they-must-include
94 gov.uk/late-commercial-payments-interest-debt-recovery/charging-interest-commercial-debt
95 gov.uk/late-commercial-payments-interest-debt-recovery/claim-debt-recovery-costs
96 gov.uk/late-commercial-payments-interest-debt-recovery
97 gov.uk/make-court-claim-for-money
98 late-payment-law.co.uk/index.html
99 paypal.com/uk/webapps/mpp/home
100 Such as **youtube.com/watch?v=ZwobgUP9ijU**
101 **csp.org.uk/public-patient/keeping-active-healthy/staying-healthy-work**
102 **nhs.uk/live-well/healthy-body/how-to-sit-correctly/**
103 **hse.gov.uk/msd/dse**
104 In England, Scotland and Wales: **gov.uk/access-to-work**; in Northern Ireland: **nidirect.gov.uk/articles/employment-support-information**

References

105 *Editing Matters*, July/August 2018, pp 13–14. ciep.uk/members/communicating/editing-matters/editing-matters-archive
106 francescocirillo.com/pages/pomodoro-technique
107 blog.ciep.uk/home-working-coworking
108 blog.ciep.uk/five-tips-coworking
109 The World Health Organization defined wellness thus in its 1946 constitution: 'Health is a state of complete physical, mental and social well-being and not merely the absence of disease or infirmity.'
110 blog.ciep.uk/customer-service
111 blog.ciep.uk/customer-service-imagination
112 blog.ciep.uk/customer-service-red-flags
113 ciep.uk/standards/complaints-and-appeals
114 blog.ciep.uk/imposter-syndrome
115 americaneditor.wordpress.com/2020/05/11/on-the-basics-scams-are-always-with-us/
116 gov.uk/report-suspicious-emails-websites-phishing
117 forums.ciep.uk/read.php?2,232718
118 google.co.uk/alerts
119 copyscape.com
120 Such as through: tineye.com
121 blog.ciep.uk/dont-panic
122 Cloud backup for Macs: **cloudwards.net/cloud-backup-for-mac** and for PCs: **uk.pcmag.com/file-syncing-and-backup/8648/the-best-online-backup-services-for-2020**
123 support.microsoft.com/en-us/help/17143/windows-10-back-up-your-files
124 support.apple.com/en-gb/HT201250
125 policybee.co.uk
126 ciep.uk/members/benefits/professional-indemnity-insurance (in the members' area)
127 ciep.uk/members/benefits (in the members' area)
128 ciep.uk/members (in the members' area under 'Your CIEP')
129 northerneditorial.co.uk/2020/05/29/how-to-prioritise-your-cpd

About the author

Sue Littleford went solo with her own freelance copyediting business, Apt Words, in March 2007. She specialises in postgraduate humanities and social sciences books, but also works on fiction and anything else that looks interesting. Prior to launching her business, she had been the payroll manager for a major government department for some 14 years. Her whole career had been markedly numbers based – both in central government and in the private sector – even though she became the go-to wordsmith everywhere she worked. She eventually decided to switch to words full-time, but has used her prior skills and experience to hone her business efficiency and effectiveness.

aptwords.co.uk

Acknowledgements

From first edition

A big thank you to the reviewers – Helen Stevens and Alison Oakes – and to the CIEP's former publications director, Steve Hammatt, who steered this guide through to fruition.

Second edition

A big thank you to all the CIEP members who contributed their advice to this and the first editions. Sadly, there wasn't room to quote it all. An equally big thank you to Liz Dalby, who project-managed this edition, and to the entire CIEP information team and Graham Hughes, the copyeditor, and Anne Gillion, the proofreader, for their inputs, refinements and outright catches. Even editors need editors.

www.ingramcontent.com/pod-product-compliance
Lightning Source LLC
Chambersburg PA
CBHW071759080526
44588CB00013B/2308